10+ COMPREHENSION PRACTICE PAPERS

Model Answers & In-Depth Guided Explanations

R. P. DAVIS

Copyright © 2022 Accolade Tuition Ltd
Published by Accolade Tuition Ltd
71-75 Shelton Street
Covent Garden
London WC2H 9JQ
www.accoladetuition.com
info@accoladetuition.com

The right of R. P. Davis to be identified as the author of this work has been asserted by him in accordance with the Copyright, Designs and Patents Act 1988.

All rights reserved. No part of this book may be reproduced in any form or by any electronic or mechanical means, including information storage and retrieval systems, without written permission from the author, except for the use of brief quotations in a book review.

ISBN 978-1-913988-26-5

FIRST EDITION
1 3 5 7 9 10 8 6 4 2

Contents

Foreword	v

Paper One: The Who? What? Where? Why? How? Paper

The Little Master of the Sky	3
Model Answers & Guidance	7

Paper Two: The Retrieval & Close Language Analysis Paper

Green Gardens	17
Model Answers & Guidance	21

Paper Three: The Retrieval and Mini Essay Paper

The Adventures of Tom Sawyer	33
Model Answers & Guidance	37

Paper Four: The Flying Blind Paper

The Tiredness of Rosabel	47
Model Answers & Guidance	51

Paper Five: The Reasoning & Reading Between the Lines Paper

Meteor Men of Mars	61
Model Answers & Guidance	65

Paper Six: The Consider Deeply Paper

The Odour of Chrysanthemums	75
Model Answers & Guidance	79

Paper Seven: The Multiple Choice Paper (Prose)

Mr. Spaceship	89
Answers & Guidance	99

Paper Eight: The Multiple Choice Paper (Poetry)

Summer-like for an Instant   123
Answers & Guidance   127

Foreword

When sitting 10+ comprehension exams at top schools, you will notice that, although all of their papers follow the same basic formula – an extract accompanied by a set of questions – the *types* of questions they ask can vary greatly. The reason for this is simple enough: a considerable number of these schools write their papers in-house, and that means you find quirks in some papers that you don't in others. And yet, for all these quirks, there is still a *huge* degree of overlap between these various papers, because ultimately these schools are all looking for a similar set of skills.

As a result, preparing for these exams is eminently possible. We simply need to identify the various types of questions that appear (including those quirky ones!), then hone the skills required to answer them.

The intention of this guide is not simply to show you what these exams tend to look like (although, as you work through it, you will inevitably get a sense of this nonetheless!). No, the intention is to go a step further, and show you how to decode the sorts of questions these 10+ comprehension papers tend to ask, and what "perfect" answers to these questions look like. Moreover, it also seeks to explain, *in detail*, how exactly the model answers provided satisfy the examiners' criteria, making it as easy as possible for students to understand how to emulate these answers.

You will notice, also, that there are a number of questions for which I have supplied alternative answers. This is because, when it comes to comprehension papers, there are frequently instances where there is not *one* correct answer – instead, there are a number of potential answers that might be worthy of scoring the marks. The alternative answers are therefore included to demonstrate how there is, very often, room for flexibility and creativity.

Now, before I press on, I feel it is important to make one crucial thing clear: this guide is explicitly aimed at those students looking to achieve at the very highest level. Many times in this guide I use sophisticated vocabulary and ideas. I promise you that my intention is *not* to intimidate. Rather, we must remember that these are competitive exams, and that the grading is administered by human beings – so it is imperative that we dazzle these examiners, and give them no choice but to fork over the marks!

Rest assured, however, that when I use these tricky words or phrases, I explain them as I go. As a result, by the time you finish working through this guide, you should have a whole new arsenal of words and phrases to help you attack papers of any kind!

How This Book Is Set Out

As mentioned, 10+ papers are incredibly varied. However, if you spend enough time and energy looking through past papers, you start to figure out what makes them tick, and notice certain patterns that emerge time and again. This book contains eight papers, each one rendered in a slightly different style. I have labelled the eight styles as follows:

1. The Who? What? Where? Why? How? Paper
2. The Retrieval & Close Language Analysis Paper
3. The Retrieval and Mini Essay Paper
4. The Flying Blind Paper
5. The Reasoning & Reading Between the Lines Paper
6. The Consider Deeply Paper
7. The Multiple Choice Paper (Prose)
8. The Multiple Choice Paper (Poetry)

The labels I've given each style should give you some indication of what the papers entail. It may well be the case that some of the 10+ comprehension papers you end up taking fit neatly into the one of these styles. However, it is just as possible that they wind up being a blend of two (or more) styles – after all, schools often tweak the style of paper they put out year on year. At any rate, I can assert with confidence that, if you are well versed in all eight styles, you will have your bases covered, and be prepared for most anything.

The questions for each paper appear twice. The first time they will appear is immediately after the extract, so that students can, if they wish, have a go at tackling the paper. They will then appear a second time, but this time accompanied by model answers and detailed guidance.

Each of the papers includes a "time guide" – that is, the amount of time one would expect to be given to complete the paper in an exam hall. If students wish to complete some of these papers as practice, I suspect this may prove useful.

Insofar as difficulty is concerned, the first six papers get increasingly tricky as the guide progresses, while the last two are both multiple choice papers and present different challenges altogether. To be clear, my intention with the more difficult papers in this edition is *not* to intimidate. On the contrary, by exposing students to the reality of what is in store, I believe it ensures that, when it actually comes to entering the exam hall, you feel far more at ease.

There is no *correct* way to use this guide. Some students will feel comfortable working through it by themselves, whereas some may prefer to have a parent at hand to act as a kind of surrogate tutor. In any case, the intention of this book is to give the reader the experience of having an experienced tutor at their beck and call.

Exam Tips

Within this book, you will find a good deal of question specific advice. However, there are a number of more general tips that it is important for any 10+ candidate to keep in mind:

- When reading the extract, don't rush. Some papers even set aside 10 minutes explicitly for reading the paper, and do not allow you to look at the questions until those 10 minutes have elapsed. This does not mean that 10 minutes is always necessary – but keep in mind that every school will expect you to read the passage very carefully.
- Read the questions carefully. It sounds obvious, I know, but you wouldn't believe how many times I have seen bright students lose marks simply because they have misread the question
- Always write in full sentences, unless you are explicitly told this is not required.
- If you are unhappy with an answer, and feel as though you must write something else, do not cross out your old answer until you have fully finished writing the new one – you may be throwing away precious marks!
- Keep quotes from the text short (unless explicitly told otherwise). As a rule of thumb, try and ensure that your quotes are no more than six or seven words in length, and preferably shorter.
- Most papers tell you how many marks a question is worth. Keep this in mind when working out how much time to spend on any given question.
- Remember: just because a question is, for instance, worth three marks, that does not necessarily mean you need to give three separate points. Of course there *are* occasions when three marks require three points, and I shall discuss those occasions in this book – but this is not *always* the case.

- Many 10+ papers give candidates blank lines on which to compose their answers. When these appear, take them seriously: they are guidelines regarding how long the examiners would like your answer to be.

Personal Note

When I talk about my academic career, I usually talk about my time spent at university: I studied English Literature & Language at UCL, then took a Masters at Cambridge University. However, a mere twenty years ago, I was in the same position that many of my readers find themselves in: eager to win a place at a top secondary school, and faced with a litany of exams. Of course, the exams have changed a fair bit since then; but what I'm trying to say is, not only have I been teaching entrance exams for many years, but I've also had first-hand experience of them – I know what they are like to live through!

Even though I now look back on that time through a rosy lens – I was offered places at all the top London private and grammar schools I sat for – I won't pretend as though it was not at times intimidating. However, I would observe that many parts of the English entrance exams, including many questions in the comprehension papers, offer rare opportunities not just to jump through hoops, but to exercise your powers of creativity. That is not to say that these exams are *fun* – my memory of them is pretty much the exact opposite – but still, it is important to at least try and embrace this creative element and enjoy the challenge.

Paper One: The Who? What? Where? Why? How? Paper

The Who? What? Where? Why? How? Paper is the most basic style in this guide, and it chiefly exercises our retrieval skills: our ability to comb through the text and accurately withdraw information. A handful of the questions in this paper will start to exercise our inference skills as well, but these are fairly few and far between.

The Little Master of the Sky
THE WHO? WHAT? WHERE? WHY? HOW? PAPER;
25 MINUTES

This extract is taken from the beginning of a short story, and explores the life of a child called Peter.

1 Peter, it seems, had at an early age dedicated his life to the pigeons. All his cares and sorrows were bound up in the lives of the birds. In fact it seemed as though he himself became birdlike. He could flap his arms to his sides and produce that same dull penetrating note that was given only to this particular species of bird when they
5 flapped their wings.

At an early age he was left without parents and managed to grow up among the horses and cows in the barns. But these larger animals were entirely out of his sphere —he did not understand them.

One day when the lad was seven years old, the village folks suddenly noticed that he
10 had an injured leg. When asked about it, all he would reply was: "The pigeons did it to me."

Luba, a farmer's cook, once told at the market-place how Peter had injured his leg. She told of how the boy stood on the roof of her master's barn flapping his arms in imitation of the birds encircling his head; how he sprang in the air in a mad attempt
15 to fly, and fell to the ground. But Luba had a reputation for being a liar, and none believed her although all enjoyed listening. "Such good imagination," they would say, after she was gone.

Peter's injury remained as he grew up, but it seemed only to add to his nimbleness. He could climb a telegraph pole sideways like a parrot walking up a stick. Once on
20 top he would swing his good leg around the cross beam and wave his hat—and from below a flight of flapping and fluttering birds would arise.

In this way he lived and grew to the age of sixteen, although his small, protruding bones and round, child-like eyes kept him looking younger. Where he slept and where he ate, all remained a mystery to the village folk.

25 He would travel about from barn to barn collecting the feed that fell from the bins of careless animals. He would sometimes travel along the back yards, twist his mouth and call to nobody in particular: "A few crumbs for the birdies, lady?" And presently through an open window a crust would fly, and with this buried in his hat he would be off.

30 The police of Millcote all knew that Peter was perfectly harmless; even though at times he would litter the streets and market-place with bread crumbs. But the pigeons of Millcote soon cleared the walks.

Only among the poor would Peter hobble about. He never ventured up the hill where the better people lived; and it is perhaps for this reason that he was seldom disturbed.

An extract adapted from Manuel Komroff's The Little Master of the Sky

---

1. Which type of bird did Peter dedicate his life to? [1]

....

2. How did Peter create a 'dull penetrating note' that sounded like the flapping of pigeon wings? [2]

....

....

3. Which two types of larger animals did Peter grow up living among in the barns? [1]

....

4. What were Peter's feelings towards the larger animals in the barn? [2]

5. How old was Peter when the people of the village realised he had an injured leg? [1]

6. According to Luba, how did Peter injure his leg? [2]

7. Why did the people of the village disbelieve Luba's version of events? [2]

8. Why do you think that the people of the village waited for Luba to depart before saying she had "Such good imagina

9. What would Peter do when he climbed to the top of a telegraph pole? [1]

10. When Peter reached sixteen-years-old, what caused him to still look younger? [2]

11. Where did Peter eat his meals? [2]

....

12. Why do you think Peter went from barn to barn collecting feed and asking for crumbs? [2]

....

....

....

13. Why do you think that the police were not concerned by the fact that Peter littered the village with crumbs? [2]

....

....

....

14. Why do you think it is that Peter was "seldom disturbed" as a result of never venturing up the hill? [3]

....

....

....

....

Model Answers & Guidance

1. Which type of bird did Peter dedicate his life to? [1]

Peter dedicated his life to pigeons.

Many 10+ papers contain 'retrieval' style questions. These basically require you to play the part of a detective, and they are all about attention to detail: the answer is lurking in the text, and it is simply a case of combing through and teasing it out.

This particular style of paper has a far greater emphasis on retrieval skills than any others in this edition – though you will notice that many papers include retrieval-style questions early on as a sort of 'warm up'.

The answer to this question can be found in the very first line of the passage, where we learn that Peter 'had at an early age dedicated his life to the pigeons'.

Note that, although brief, my model answer above nevertheless constitutes a full sentence. As a rule of thumb, *always* write in full sentences, unless you're explicitly told it is not necessary!

2. How did Peter create a 'dull penetrating note' that sounded like the flapping of pigeon wings? [2]

Peter created a 'dull penetrating note' by flapping his arms up and down against his sides.

Again, we are dealing with a retrieval-style question. This time the answer is lurking at lines 3-4, where we learn that Peter could 'flap his arms to his sides' in order to 'produce that same dull penetrating note' that pigeons create when they flap their wings.

The skill required is nearly identical to the skill being tested in the previous question. However, you'll notice that this time the question is worth two marks as opposed to just one. This largely reflects the fact it is ever so slightly harder – the answer this time is not simply in the opening sentence, and the phrase 'this particular species' at line 4, which is used to refer to the pigeons, may confuse some candidates.

It is important to note that, just because the question is worth an extra mark, this does not mean you have to make two separate points. I know this may seem confusing, but as you work through this guide, it will become increasingly easy to recognise when the exam paper is expecting you to produce multiple arguments/points.

3. Which two types of larger animals did Peter grow up living among in the barns? [1]

Peter grew up living among horses and cows in the barns.

The answer to this one can be found at lines 6 to 7, where we are informed that Peter 'managed to grow up among the horses and cows in the barns'.

You must mention both horses *and* cows to score the mark: after all, the question is explicitly asking you for *two* types of animals.

4. What were Peter's feelings towards the larger animals in the barn? [2]

Peter found it a struggle not only to empathise with these larger animals, but also to comprehend them. This is because he felt as though he belonged to a different sort of metaphorical world to these larger animals.[1]

This question is testing our retrieval skills again, yet is ever so slightly trickier than the previous questions.

At lines 7 to 8, we are told about Peter's feelings towards the larger animals: 'these larger animals were entirely out of his sphere—he did not understand them'.

The first mark up for grabs is for acknowledging that Peter did not understand / comprehend these larger animals. To score the second mark, however, you have to demonstrate some understanding of the phrase 'entirely out of his sphere'. This expression implies that Peter exists in a different metaphorical world to these larger animals, and this impedes his understanding of them.[2] If a candidate merely repeats the phrase 'out of his sphere', without attempting to explain what this means, they will not score this second mark.

5. How old was Peter when the people of the village realised he had an injured leg? [1]

Peter was seven-years-old when the people of the village realised that he had an injured leg.

A straightforward retrieval question: the candidate will score the mark for acknowledging that Peter was seven-years-old when the village realised he was injured. The answer is lurking at lines 9-10, which reads as follows: 'One day when the lad was seven years old, the village folks suddenly noticed that he had an injured leg.'

6. According to Luba, how did Peter injure his leg? [2]

In Luba's telling, Peter injured his leg by flinging himself off the roof of Luba's boss's barn. Luba asserts that, when Peter had flung himself, he had been attempting to copy the birds that had been flying above his head.

You are likely getting the measure of the Who? What? Where? Why? How? Paper by this point: it is a workout for our retrieval skills!

This time, the details we are looking for can be found between lines 12 and 15, where Luba gives her account of how Peter wound up injured. One mark is for acknowledging that Peter leapt off Luba's boss's barn. The second mark is for mentioning that he did so while attempting to mimic/imitate the birds that had been flying overhead.

7. Why did the people of the village disbelieve Luba's version of events? [2]

The people of the village disbelieved Luba's version of events because she had a track-record for telling untruths.

The answer for this question can be found at lines 15 to 16, where we are told that 'Luba had a reputation for being a liar, and none believed her'. In short, the examiner wants us to mention that the village people disbelieved Luba because she was considered to be a liar.

This is another occasion where two discrete points are not required to score the mark.[3] Rather, the examiner has simply deemed that this retrieval question is slightly more difficult due to the vocabulary the author uses / the fact the answer is slightly more hidden away within the passage.

8. Why do you think that the people of the village waited for Luba to depart before saying she had "Such good imagination"? [2]

The people of the village likely waited for Luba to depart before remarking on her imagination because this comment insinuates that the story Luba has told is not true – that it is a product of her imagination. Since this could be construed as an insult, the people of the village decided to not say it to Luba's face: perhaps to spare her feelings, and perhaps to avoid confrontation.[4]

For the first time, this paper is categorically asking the candidate to move beyond simple retrieval. Instead, we are being asked to make an inference – to draw a conclusion that is not spelt out explicitly in the text already.

The first mark is for acknowledging that the phrase 'such good imagination' is an articulation of the villagers' belief that Luba's account is a lie – a figment of her imagination. The second mark is for acknowledging that they did not wish to call her a liar to her face, with a sensible explanation as to why they would not want to do so (for example, it would be offensive, or would potentially start a fight).

9. What would Peter do when he climbed to the top of a telegraph pole? [1]

Peter, when he climbed to the top of a telegraph pole, would wrap his uninjured leg around the horizontal element then wave his hat around.

This question is once again exercising our retrieval skills.

Although this question is worth one mark, the candidate must mention both the fact that Peter, on reaching the top of the pole, would: a) wrap his uninjured leg around the cross beam/horizontal beam; and b) wave his hat around. If a candidate fails to mention both of these details, they will not score the mark!

10. When Peter reached sixteen-years-old, what caused him to still look younger? [2]

When Peter hit sixteen, he still looked as though he was younger than this as a result of his small, protuberant bones and his large, youthful eyes.[5]

Like the previous question, this retrieval question requires you to pick out two details. However, this time, there is one mark at stake for each of these two details. The two factors that caused Peter to look younger are: a) his large, child-like eyes; and b) his protruding bones. If a candidate mentions one of these factors, but not the other, they will be capped at one mark.

11. Where did Peter eat his meals? [2]

The reader does not learn where Peter ate his meals; rather, we are informed that this was a mystery to the people of the village.

This question appears at first glance to again be exercising our retrieval skills, but is in fact slightly trickier than others we have encountered so far.

Looking closely at the passage, we are in fact never told where Peter eats. However, at lines 23-24, we are told the following: 'Where he slept and where he ate, all remained a mystery to the village folk.'

Given that there is no other feasible answer, we have to infer that the examiner wants us to seize on this moment in the passage and state that we are in fact not told where Peter ate his meals, and that it is a mystery to both us and the people of the village. By doing so, we will pick up both marks!

"Trick questions" of this kind are rare, but do appear from time to time in 10+ papers. My advice: keep a cool head and make sure you read the passage carefully. This will help you identify questions of this kind – that is, questions that in fact have no definitive answer!

12. Why do you think Peter went from barn to barn collecting feed and asking for crumbs? [2]

I believe Peter collected feed from barns and begged for crumbs because he plans to feed these provisions to the pigeons – the animal with which Peter is obsessed. When Peter shouts out 'A few crumbs for the birdies, lady?', he strongly hints that he is scavenging on the pigeons' behalf.

There is also a possibility that Peter collects some of this food for himself; after all, it would appear that the parentless Peter is not a wealthy individual, and thus it is reasonable to think he might need to scavenge for food.[6]

This question represents another foray beyond mere retrieval, because the reader is not told definitively why Peter goes from barn to barn collecting feed and crumbs, although we are given a strong hint.

At line 27 (which appears in the paragraph narrating the way Peter collects feed and crumbs), we are told that Peter would shout out the phrase 'A few crumbs for the birdies, lady?'. As a result, it is reasonable to take Peter at his word and argue that Peter is collecting food for the birds. If a candidate mentions this quote, and asserts that Peter is collecting for the birds, they will score both marks.

You will notice, however, that I have also included a second potential reason why Peter collects the feed and crumbs – namely, that it is potentially to feed himself. I likely would have already scored the two marks with my previous paragraph; but by including a second feasible (and well-argued reason), I am attempting to dazzle the examiner and win them over to my side. Remember: examiners are human beings. We want to impress them, and to make them as disposed as possible to give us marks as they move through our exam script. So why not occasionally go above and beyond?!

It is also important to note that if a candidate did *not* mention the notion that Peter was collecting food for the birds, and argued only that Peter was collecting food for himself, they could still conceivably score both marks. After all, we are never told definitively that the food is for the birds (Peter could be lying!), and thus the examiner would still reward this alternative, yet entirely feasible, line of argument (provided it was argued well!).

<u>13. Why do you think that the police were not concerned by the fact that Peter littered the village with crumbs? [2]</u>

The police were not concerned by Peter littering the village with crumbs because the mess was very temporary: the pigeons would soon eat the crumbs that Peter had left behind.

Although we are being asked to put forward a reason, the skills being tested only go slightly beyond retrieval.

At lines 31-32, we read that 'the pigeons of Millcote soon cleared the walks' of any crumbs Peter left littered around. This detail comes just after the assertion that the police thought Peter was 'harmless…even though at times he would litter the streets and market-place with bread crumbs'.

Even though the logic is not explicitly spelt out, the way these ideas are ordered strongly suggest a causality – namely, that it was because the pigeons dealt with Peter's littering that he was deemed harmless by the police. Any candidate who is able to intuit this causality will score both marks.[7]

14. Why do you think it is that Peter was "seldom disturbed" as a result of never venturing up the hill? [3]

> **We learn in the final sentence that 'the better people' (in other words, the wealthier, better-off people) live up the hill. We can infer that by avoiding this up-hill neighbourhood, Peter ensured that he did not make himself a nuisance to the village's wealthier contingent – a contingent arguably more likely to find the idiosyncratic Peter a nuisance in the first-place, and more likely to have the means and connections to hassle Peter in retaliation.[8][9]**

This is the trickiest question in this paper, and the only one that is worth more than two marks.

In short, it requires the reader to look beyond the facts of the narrative and demonstrate a deeper understanding.

The first challenge is to decipher the phrase 'the better people', which is used to describe the people who live on top of the hill. Candidates need to make the inference that this refers to the wealthier villagers / those with more power or education. By correctly deciphering this phrase, the candidate will score one of the three marks up for grabs.

To score the other two marks, the candidate needs to explain how, by making sure not to bother the wealthier people of the village, Peter ensures that he is not hassled – because the wealthier people have more power to wield against Peter (perhaps by setting the police on him). Candidates must fully explain this notion to score these two further marks.

1. When I write 'different sort of metaphorical world', I do not mean that Peter literally exists in a different world to these animals. Rather, I am saying that Peter understands these animals so little that it is almost as though he occupies a different world to them, even though they of course quite literally exist in the same world. This is what I mean by the word 'metaphorical' – this indicates that I am not talking literally!
2. To impede something or someone is to hinder or obstruct that something or someone.
3. The word 'discrete' here means separate. This is not to be confused with the word discreet, which means subtle/inconspicuous.
4. A confrontation refers to a fight, or an argument, or some other kind of hostilities.
5. Protuberant means something akin to protruding or bulging
6. To scavenge means to hunt around for scraps that others might have left behind, or might not want.
7. To intuit something is to work something out using one's intuition!
8. The word contingent refers to a group of people who represent a wider population.
9. If something is idiosyncratic, it means it is unusual.

Paper Two: The Retrieval & Close Language Analysis Paper

Although this paper has plenty in common with the previous style of paper – that is to say, it also exercises our retrieval skills in a big way – it also pushes us further by asking us to also engage in close language analysis. This is when we need to hone in on specific language used by the author and discuss its effects on the reader, and these sorts of questions require students to operate at a more advanced level.

Green Gardens
THE RETRIEVAL & CLOSE LANGUAGE ANALYSIS
PAPER; 30 MINUTES

This extract is taken from the start of a short story. In it, Daphne pays a visit to the gardens at Green Gardens Manor.

---

1   Daphne was singing to herself when she came through that painted gate (so like a portal to Eden!) in the back wall. She was singing partly because it was June, and Devon, and she was seventeen, and partly because she had caught a breath-taking glimpse of herself in the long mirror as she had flashed through the hall at home, and
5   it seemed almost too good to be true that the radiant small person in the green muslin frock with the wreath of golden hair bound about her head, and the sea-blue eyes laughing back at her, was really Miss Daphne Chiltern. Incredible, incredible luck to look like that, half mythical creature, half film-star. She danced down the turf path that glistened like the sea and approached the herb-garden, swinging her great wicker
10 basket and singing like a small mad thing.

The song stopped as abruptly as though some one had struck it from her lips. A strange man was kneeling by the beehive in the herb-garden. He was looking at her over his shoulder, at once startled and amused, and she saw that he was wearing a rather shabby tweed suit and that his face was remarkably freckled against his close-
15 cropped, tawny hair. He smiled, his teeth a strong flash of white.

"Hello!" he greeted her, in a tone at once casual and friendly.

Daphne returned the smile uncertainly. "Hello," she replied gravely.

20 The strange man rose easily to his feet, and she saw that he was very tall and carried his head rather splendidly, like the young bronze Greek statue in Uncle Roland's study at home. But his eyes—his eyes were strange—quite dark and burned out. The rest of him looked young and vivid and adventurous—but his eyes looked as though the adventure were over, though they were still **questing**.

"Were you looking for any one?" she asked, and the man shook his head, laughing.

"No one in particular, unless it was you."

25 Daphne's soft brow darkened. "It couldn't possibly have been me," she said in a rather stately small voice, "because, you see, I don't know you. Perhaps you didn't know that there is no one living in Green Gardens Manor now?"

"Oh, yes, I knew. The Fanes have left for South Asia, haven't they?"

30 "Sir Harry left two weeks ago, because he had to see the old governor before he sailed, but Lady Audrey only left last week. She had to close the London house, too, so there was a great deal to do."

"I see. And so Green Gardens is **deserted**?"

"It is sold," said Daphne, with a small quaver in her voice, "just this afternoon. I came over to say good-by to it, and to get some mint and lavender from the garden."

An extract adapted from Frances Noyes Hart's Green Gardens

---

1. There are three similes in the opening paragraph. In the chart below, list all three things that are being compared to something, and the three things they are being compared to. [3]

An entity within the opening paragraph	What it is compared to?

2. From the first paragraph, explain in full sentences, in your own words, [4]

   a) two reasons why Daphne was in a good mood, and

   b) two different ways she showed her good mood.

3. Look at lines 18 to 22. Choose a word or phrase from this section of the passage which suggests that Daphne thinks the man is attractive. Write it below and explain why you have chosen it. [2]

4. Explain the meaning of the following two words, as they are used in the passage. (They are in bold in the passage.) [2]

   a) questing

   b) deserted

5. The author portrays the man as being unusual. Find two examples of this in the passage. [4]

   - Write them below.
   - Explain in what way they make the man seem unusual.

6. Why was Daphne at Green Gardens Manor? (Answer in a proper sentence, in your own words) [1]

7. From what you have read in this passage, what impressions do you form of Daphne's character? Give examples from the text to support the points that you make. [4]

Model Answers & Guidance

1. There are three similes in the opening paragraph. In the chart below, list all three things that are being compared to something, and the three things they are being compared to. [3]

An entity within the opening paragraph	What it is compared to?
the painted gate	a portal to Eden
the turf path	the sea
Miss Daphne Chiltern	a small, mad thing

While this question exercises retrieval skills, it is slightly trickier than most we encountered in the previous paper. Put briefly, we need to comb the opening paragraph for the three similes we have been told are lurking within. Then, for each simile, we need to identify both: a) what the simile is being used to describe; and b) what the simile is making a comparison to. Since there are three marks at stake, we know that there is one mark available for each simile successfully identified.

Remember, similes are comparisons that make use of either the word 'as' or 'like.'

In this passage's opening paragraph, the author uses the word 'like' to formulate all three of the similes that appear.

The first simile can be found in the following quotation: 'she came through that painted gate (so like a portal to Eden!) in the back wall'. Here the 'painted gate' is being likened to 'a portal to Eden'. The slightly tricky thing is that the author has placed the simile in brackets, so some students may miss it.

To score the mark, you need to get both the left and right-hand sides of the table correct.

The second simile can be found in the following quotation: 'She danced down the turf path that glistened like the sea'. Here the author is comparing the 'turf path' to 'the sea'. It is the way that both glistened that inspires the author to draw the comparison; but we are not being asked about that. Rather, we just need to list what the simile is describing, and what the simile is invoking for a comparison.

The final simile is in fact in the same sentence. Let's look at the sentence in its entirety: 'She danced down the turf path that glistened like the sea and approached the herb-garden, swinging her great wicker basket and singing like a small mad thing.'

This time, Daphne herself is being compared to 'a small mad thing.' It is ambiguous whether it's the way she is swinging her great wicker basket or the way she is singing (or both!) that makes her seem similar to 'a small mad thing'. But for the sake of this question, we need not worry about that. We simply need to list what the subject of the simile is (Daphne herself), and what she is being compared to ('a small mad thing').

If a candidate in the final left-hand column wrote 'Daphne's singing' or 'Daphne's swinging of the basket', instead of just Daphne, they will still be awarded the mark. However, if they wrote just 'singing' or just 'swinging of the basket', the candidate will not score the third and final mark.

2. From the first paragraph, explain in full sentences, in your own words, [4]

a) two reasons why Daphne was in a good mood, and

The first reason Daphne was in a good mood was because she was in a beautiful place (Devon), at a beautiful time of year (summer), at a wonderful point of time in her life (she is seventeen). This sense of fortuitous time and place is the first key to her good mood.[1] The second is her pleasure in her own appearance: she had, just earlier in the day,

inspected herself in the mirror, and had felt overwhelmingly blessed to have been born so beautiful.

Before anything else, let's stop for the moment and consider the phrase 'in your own words' that we see in this question. Questions that ask you to put things 'in your own words' are another perennial favourite of 10+ question writers. The basic premise is that, if you are able to explain an element of the passage in your own words, you demonstrate that you truly understand it.

As the phraseology of the question implies, it is important to try as best you can to avoid the vocabulary used in the extract – you can see that my explanation, leaving aside a tiny handful of words, has been written with entirely fresh vocabulary.

Now let's dive into the question itself.

There are two marks up for grabs in part (a) of this question: one for each reason the candidate is able to offer.

Some students will reasonably argue that what I present as just one reason for Daphne's good mood – namely, a sense of 'fortuitous time and place' – ought really to be considered three separate reasons: a) the fact Daphne is in Devon; b) the fact it is summer; and c) the fact she is seventeen. And indeed, many examiners may well award the full two marks to candidates who bring up any two of these.

So: why did I clump them together? For one thing, the author also clumps these reasons together, so it felt organic for me to do the same. For another thing, I knew the text included still one more justification for Daphne's good mood – namely, her sense of good fortune at her own good looks – and I knew I could use this as my "second" reason

But in fact the key thing motivating my approach was a desire to go above and beyond. By clumping those three reasons together, and then mentioning still one more, I am showing the examiner that I have picked up on *all* the reasons Daphne was feeling happy. I am giving the examiner absolutely zero room to dock me marks!

<u>b) two different ways she showed her good mood.</u>

The first and most obvious externalisation of Daphne's good mood is her singing: this is mentioned multiple times, and she even acknowledges explicitly to herself that it was intimately linked to her buoyant mood.[2] Another externalisation of her good mood is the carefree way she moved her body: not only did she dance as she walked, but she also rocked her basket as she did so.

Section (b) is also worth two marks.

The most obvious way in which Daphne exhibited her good mood was her singing, which is mentioned a number of times in the opening paragraph.

Students can score the second mark either by mentioning the fact that Daphne was dancing, or the fact she was swinging her basket (or both, as I have done in my answer!).

Significantly, we are never told explicitly that Daphne's singing/dancing/basket swinging indicates a good mood. Rather, this is something the examiner is expecting us to *infer*.

3. Look at lines 18 to 22. Choose a word or phrase from this section of the passage which suggests that Daphne thinks the man is attractive. Write it below and explain why you have chosen it. [2]

> **A phrase that suggests that Daphne finds the man attractive is the following simile: 'like the young bronze Greek statue'. By likening the man – or, more specifically, the way he carries his head – to a Greek statue, Daphne is suggesting that he has the sort of perfect, idealised demeanour one associates with classical art.[3] The word 'young' also suggests that Daphne sees a virility in the man that could be construed as attractive.[4]**

This question is requiring us to exercise a new skill: namely, close language analysis.

This is testing our ability to drill into the language an author uses and to dissect the impact of their choices.

The first mark is for picking a quote that suggests that Daphne thinks the man is attractive. The second is for capably dissecting the quote chosen and explaining how it communicates the fact Daphne finds the man attractive. As you can see, I decided to grab the simile that likens the man to a Greek statue – 'like the young bronze Greek statue' – and proceeded to look at how the allusion to 'Greek' art links the man to classical conceptions of beauty, as well as how the word 'young' suggests an appealing virility.

However, it is important to note that the way I analyse this quote is not the only valid way of doing so. For instance, a candidate could also have analysed instead the word 'bronze' and discussed how, by invoking a precious metal that is generally considered beautiful and decorative, the author further suggests that the man is aesthetically pleasing: after all, it hints that the man has attractive/appealing skin-coloration. In short, candidates will get credit for any argument that is sensible, coherent, and answers the question.

Of course, it is also the case that there are a number of other quotes a candidate might have picked to analyse instead. For instance, we might have picked the phrase 'young and vivid and adventurous'. To demonstrate how there's more than one way to score the marks in this question, here's an alternative model answer for this alternative quote:

> **A phrase that suggests Daphne finds the man attractive would be as follows: 'young and vivid and adventurous'. This list of adjectives suggest that Daphne sees various attractive traits in this man: 'young' hints at virility; 'vivid', a more abstract word, suggests a kind of compelling aura, an air of charismatic intensity; and 'adventurous' hints not only at a level of physical fitness, but also an attractive lack of inhibition in his demeanour.**

<u>4. Explain the meaning of the following two words, as they are used in the passage. (They are in bold in the passage.) [2]</u>

<u>a) questing</u>

> **The word 'questing' means roaming or adventuring.**

<u>b) deserted</u>

> **The word 'deserted' means unoccupied or empty.**

This style of question – that is, one that asks the candidate to give a definition of a word in light of its context – is a time-honoured favourite of 10+ examiners. In this paper, the candidate is presented with just two words; however, other papers present students with a far longer list.

Again, on this occasion, I am opting to use full sentences, since the exam paper has not given me permission to do otherwise.

When you are offering your definition, make sure you are using the same tense as the word you are defining. A good question to ask yourself is: would the word I'm using fit seamlessly into the passage if I were to swap it in for the word I'm defining? If the answer is yes, you are on the right lines.

If you are uncertain of the meaning of any word, read the sentence within which it appears carefully – and, if need be, the sentences immediately preceding and proceeding it. In doing so, you might realise that you can make a decent educated guess. Remember, it is always better to make an educated guess than it is to leave the answer sheet blank.

5. The author portrays the man as being unusual. Find two examples of this in the passage. [4]

- Write them below.
- Explain in what way they make the man seem unusual.

One example of the man being portrayed as unusual is the description of his eyes, and how his eyes clash with his overarching air. The reader is told not only that his eyes were 'strange' – a synonym for unusual – but also 'quite dark and burned out'. The word 'dark' here seems to be metaphorical: whereas his general appearance is 'vivid' and youthful, his eyes stand out for their seeming lack of vividness; for the fact that they have in fact seemingly lost a prior vividness ('burned out').

Another way the man is presented as unusual is through the description of him as being 'at once startled and amused'. To be startled is generally to be placed uncomfortably off-kilter, and perhaps even slightly afraid, whereas to be amused generally suggests a relaxed, laid-back demeanour. That the man paradoxically yokes these two qualities is a striking feat, and certainly functions to portray him as unusual.[5]

Here we have another close language analysis question – this one centring on the ways in which the man in the passage is presented as unusual. However, this question is phrased slightly differently to the previous close language question, since it is asking us for two examples, not two quotes. Yet it is important not to be thrown off by this: it will still be essential to bring in quotes when putting forward your two examples.

There are two marks at stake for each relevant example a candidate brings up, though a candidate will only score these marks if they back their examples up with quotes from the passage. There are a further two marks at stake for explaining these examples / interacting with the quotes – one mark for each separate explanation.

The first example I pick out in my model answer is the description of the man's eyes as being 'quite dark and burned out', and, crucially, the way his eyes clash with his overall youthfulness; I then explain how this discrepancy is used to present the man as strange.[6]

The second example I pick out is the description of the man as being 'at once startled and amused'. I then score my explanation mark by discussing how being 'startled' is a state we might consider to be at odds with being 'amused' – and how the author, by having the man appear to embody these contrary states at once, is able to present the man as unusual.

6. Why was Daphne at Green Gardens Manor? (Answer in a proper sentence, in your own words) [1]

Daphne was at Green Gardens Manor because the owners have sold the property; so, given that she would very soon not be able to visit, Daphne decided to visit the one last time in order to bid the place farewell and pick some flowers.

Again, we have the phrase 'in your own words', so we must make a conscious effort to write our response using vocabulary that largely differs from the vocabulary the author uses.

In short, to score the mark, you need to acknowledge the key reason why Daphne was at Green Gardens Manor: the fact that the owners were selling it, and that she was therefore visiting to bid the place a final farewell. You need to mention both the fact it was due to be sold *and* Daphne's intention to say goodbye to score the mark.

You will also notice that I mention that she was there to pick the flowers. If a candidate just wrote this in isolation, the examiner is unlikely to award the mark. However, I decided to include the detail in order to impress the examiner with my alertness to detail (another example of me going above and beyond!).

7. From what you have read in this passage, what impressions do you form of Daphne's character? Give examples from the text to support the points that you make. [4]

A key impression we form of Daphne is that she is self-involved, albeit in an innocent enough way. The opening paragraph gives a strong sense of Daphne being self-involved: she meditates at length at the 'incredible luck' of being as beautiful as she is, and how 'it seemed almost too good to be true'. That this meditation stems from a 'glimpse' in a 'long mirror' is telling, since the act of looking in the mirror is a potent symbol of self-involvement. Later in the passage, Daphne tells the man that he cannot have been looking for her 'because, you see, I don't know you'. For Daphne, it is *her* point of view – in other words, whether or not she knows him, not vice versa – that is all-important.

Another key facet to Daphne is her cautiousness.[7] **On encountering the man, although she returns his smile, she does so 'uncertainly' – which nods to her desire to cautiously withhold judgement – and her tone is far more guarded: whereas the man is 'casual and friendly', Daphne's tone is 'grave'. Moreover, there are continued hints that a residual cautiousness persists in Daphne throughout her interaction – whether it be the way her 'soft brow darkened' in scepticism, or the defensive 'stately' voice she uses to address him shortly after.**

The question is phrased in a way that makes it seem almost as though it is looking for an essay in response. However, this particular paper has only set aside four marks, so we know that we do not need to deliver a full-blown essay.

Instead, it is reasonable to conclude that we need to come up with two strong, well-developed points, each backed up by quotes from the extract.

In my view, this particular style of question – one that asks us to consider the passage as a whole, and to comment on a character or an idea – lends itself to a thematic approach. What do I mean by this? Basically, I'm suggesting that each of your paragraphs should be organised by a different concept that answers the question.

For this question, I wanted two concepts, so I put together an incredibly short plan before writing my response.

- Theme 1: Daphne is innocently self-involved.
- Theme 2: Daphne is cautious.

Armed with this short plan, I had a clear idea of what I would be arguing.

We will encounter questions in this guide that are similar to this, but are worth far more marks, and thus require somewhat longer plans, *and* somewhat longer responses. But remember, papers differ from school to school, so it is entirely possible that you get a question like this – that is, one that feels as though it ought to require a full-blown essay – but is in fact worth a smaller number of marks.

Also, it's important to note that the two themes I've pitched above are not definitive. In other words, a candidate might have had different theme – for instance, that Daphne is carefree, or that she is self-important – and that candidate's answer could just as readily won them the four marks. Questions of this kind leave room for a degree of creativity. The key thing is for the examiner to see that you have the ability to come up with mature ideas, and then to back these ideas up convincingly with evidence.

If a candidate only discusses one impression of Daphne, they will cap themselves at two marks. It is imperative that candidates include at least two strong ideas to score above two marks.

---

1. If something is fortuitous, it means it came about through fortunate circumstances
2. An externalisation is something that outwardly demonstrates an internal emotional state. Crying, for instance, might be considered an externalisation of sadness.
3. Classical art refers to art that comes from, or seeks to emulate, the ancient civilisations of Greece and/or Rome.
4. To be virile is to be young and energetic, and hints also at sexual potency.
5. A paradox is when you have two contradictory ideas in tandem; so, in this instance, the idea of both being 'amused' and 'startled' is paradoxical. Paradoxes come in all sorts of shapes and sizes. Another example of a paradox is the idea that God might make a stone so heavy that even he could not move it. The immovability of the stone clashes with the idea of God as an infinitely powerful being.
    To yoke two things together is to bring them together / join them together.
6. A discrepancy is a gap or difference between two things.
7. A facet of an object is a face or side of that object. We can use the word metaphorically, however, and talk about facets of people's personalities.

Paper Three: The Retrieval and Mini Essay Paper

As the name suggests, we will again be contending with retrieval-based questions in this paper. However, unlike the previous two papers, this one finishes with an essay style question that will stretch our analytical skills further. Yet this is not the only way this paper will push us into new territory: it will also test our ability to explain, and our ability to understand choices the author has made to do with punctuation and formatting. This may sound intimidating, but don't despair: we will be taking it all step by step!

The Adventures of Tom Sawyer
THE RETRIEVAL AND MINI ESSAY PAPER; 30 MINUTES

This is a short extract from a novel. It is set in the 1840s and explores the life of a young boy called Tom Sawyer, who lives by the Mississippi River in America. In this passage, we join Tom on a Monday morning.

1   Monday morning found Tom Sawyer miserable. Monday morning always found him so—because it began another week's slow suffering in school. He generally began that day with wishing he had had no intervening holiday, it made the going into captivity and fetters again so much more <u>odious</u>.

5   Tom lay thinking. Presently it occurred to him that he wished he was sick; then he could stay home from school. Here was a vague possibility. He investigated his system. No ailment was found, and he investigated again. This time he thought he could detect cold-like symptoms, and he began to encourage them with considerable hope. But they soon grew feeble, and presently died wholly away. He reflected further.

10 Suddenly he discovered something. One of his upper front teeth was loose. This was lucky; he was about to begin to groan, when it occurred to him that if he came into court with that argument, his aunt would pull it out, and that would hurt. So he thought he would hold the tooth in reserve for the present, and seek further. Nothing offered for some little time, and then he remembered hearing the doctor tell about a

15 certain thing that laid up a patient for two or three weeks and threatened to make him lose a finger. So the boy eagerly drew his sore toe from under the sheet and held

it up for inspection. But now he did not know the necessary symptoms. However, it seemed well worth while to chance it, so he fell to groaning with considerable spirit.

But Sid slept on unconscious.

20 Tom groaned louder, and fancied that he began to feel pain in the toe.

No result from Sid.

Tom was panting with his <u>exertions</u> by this time. He took a rest and then swelled himself up and fetched a succession of admirable groans.

Sid snored on.

25 Tom was aggravated. He said, "Sid, Sid!" and shook him. This course worked well, and Tom began to groan again. Sid yawned, stretched, then brought himself up on his elbow with a snort, and began to stare at Tom. Tom went on groaning. Sid said:

"Tom! Say, Tom!" [No response.] "Here, Tom! TOM! What is the matter, Tom?" And he shook him and looked in his face anxiously.

30 Tom moaned out:

"Oh, don't, Sid. Don't <u>joggle</u> me."

"Why, what's the matter, Tom? I must call auntie."

"No—never mind. It'll be over by and by, maybe. Don't call anybody."

"But I must! *Don't* groan so, Tom, it's awful. How long you been this way?"

35 "Hours. Ouch! Oh, don't stir so, Sid, you'll kill me."

"Tom, why didn't you wake me sooner? Oh, Tom, *don't!* It makes my flesh crawl to hear you. Tom, what is the matter?"

"I forgive you everything, Sid. [Groan.] Everything you've ever done to me. When I'm gone—"

40 "Oh, Tom, you ain't dying, are you? Don't, Tom—oh, don't. Maybe—"

"I forgive everybody, Sid. [Groan.] Tell 'em so, Sid. And Sid, you give my window-sash and my cat with one eye to that new girl that's come to town, and tell her—"

But Sid had snatched his clothes and gone. Tom was suffering in reality, now, so handsomely was his imagination working, and so his groans had gathered quite a 45 <u>genuine</u> tone.

Sid flew downstairs and said:

"Oh, Aunt Polly, come! Tom's dying!"

"Dying!"

"Yes'm. Don't wait—come quick!"

50 "Rubbage! I don't believe it!"

But she fled upstairs, nevertheless, with Sid and cousin Mary at her heels. And her face grew white, too, and her lip trembled. When she reached the bedside she gasped out:

"You, Tom! Tom, what's the matter with you?"

55 "Oh, auntie, I'm—"

"What's the matter with you—what is the matter with you, child?"

"Oh, auntie, my sore toe's mortified!"

The old lady sank down into a chair and laughed a little, then cried a little, then did both together. This <u>restored</u> her and she said:

60 "Tom, what a turn you did give me. Now you shut up that nonsense and climb out of this."

An extract adapted from Mark Twain's The Adventures of Tom Sawyer

1. Tom has three relatives, all of whom are mentioned in this passage. What are their names? [1]

2. Using paragraphs 1 and 2 to help you, explain why Tom decided to start making a fuss of his sore toe. [3]

3. Explain using your own words why Tom shook Sid (line 25). [2]

4. Choose two lively verbs from between lines 43 and 46 that are used to describe Sid's reactions to Tom's comments. [2]

5. What is the effect of the author occasionally using square brackets in this passage? [2]

6. The following words are underlined in the passage. Suggest another word or phrase to explain the meaning of each one, as it is used in the passage. [6]

   a) Odious

   b) Exertions

c) Joggle

d) Genuine

e) Restored

7. Why does Tom's Aunt both laugh and cry at the end of the passage? [4]

8. Think about the passage as a whole. How does the author make the passage comical for the reader? [6]

Think about how Tom behaves, how Sid and his Aunt react, and our feelings about the various characters. Use your own words but also refer to evidence in the passage to support what you say.

Model Answers & Guidance

1. Tom has three relatives, all of whom are mentioned in this passage. What are their names? [1]

Tom Sawyer's three relatives are called Polly, Sid and Mary.

To score the mark, you need to name all three of Tom's relatives.

We know that Tom's aunt is called Polly: she is named by Sid at line 47 ("Oh, Aunt Polly, come! Tom's dying!").

That Sid and Tom share an aunt is a clear indication that they, too, are related; therefore, Sid is the second name the examiner is looking for.

At line 51, we are told how Polly 'fled upstairs…with Sid and cousin Mary at her heels.' Mary is explicitly described as a cousin, and thus we know that Mary is the third and final name the examiner is looking for.

2. Using paragraphs 1 and 2 to help you, explain why Tom decided to start making a fuss of his sore toe. [3]

The overarching reason Tom makes a fuss of his sore toe is because he hates school – the passage is set on a Monday morning and Tom believes that, by feigning an ailment, he might be able to 'stay home from school'. Tom decides to fuss about his toe in particular due to an absence of other

> viable options: he lacks 'cold-like symptoms' that might convince Aunt Polly he is ill, and he fears that focusing on his loose tooth will only cause Polly to painfully yank it out.
>
> **Finally, Tom decides to make a fuss of his toe because he remembers hearing a doctor discussing a patient who, as a result of a sore finger, was forced to rest 'for two or three weeks', and thus Tom hopes that complaining about his toe might yield a similar result.**

To score all three marks here, a candidate needs to pinpoint *all* the reasons Tom chose to start making a fuss of his sore toe: a) he wanted an excuse to avoid attending school; b) he believed he had no better excuse to put forward; and c) he had heard a doctor discussing a patient who had been incapacitated by a sore finger, which gave him reason to think that fussing about his toe might yield results.

A candidate will score one mark for each one of these reasons they cover.

3. Explain using your own words why Tom shook Sid (line 25). [2]

> **Above all, Tom shook Sid because Tom wanted to wake Sid up. To add credibility to his faux sickness, Tom had wanted to appear too sick to even get out of bed to alert Aunt Polly, and thus Tom needed Sid to wake up so he could witness Tom's state and raise the alarm.[1] Tom chose this particular method of waking Sid up – namely, shaking him – because Tom had already tried and failed to wake Sid up by groaning loudly ('a succession of admirable groans').**

Again we have a question that contains the phrase 'using your own words'; so, like last time, we need to ensure that our response here is largely using different vocabulary and wording to the wording used in the extract. If a candidate answers the question correctly, but uses barely any of their own wording or vocab, they are in danger of scoring zero marks.

The two points the examiner wants to see regarding Tom's motivation for shaking Sid are as follows: 1) Tom needed to rouse Sid from his sleep so that Sid could then witness Tom's illness and tell Aunt Polly; and 2) Tom chose specifically to shake Sid as the method to wake Sid up because his groans had failed to do the job.

One mark is at stake for each of these two points.

4. Choose two lively verbs from between lines 43 and 46 that are used to describe Sid's reactions to Tom's comments. [2]

Two lively words that the author uses to describe Sid's reaction to Tom's comments are 'snatched' and 'flew'.

A verb is a 'doing' word. This is a fairly straightforward question, and the examiner merely wants us to pick out two verbs from between lines 43 and 46 that help communicate Sid's lively reaction to Tom's comments.

The two verbs I've picked out are the most obvious choices. The only other valid verb a student might have picked is the word 'gone'.

One mark is on offer for each correct verb (with a maximum of two marks available in all).

5. What is the effect of the author occasionally using square brackets in this passage? [2]

The author uses square brackets during dialogue in order to feed the reader additional details in a quick, unobtrusive way. This technique, which resembles stage directions in a play, allows the reader to stay engrossed in the dialogue, while also giving them snippets of information that enhances the dialogue – for instance, the standalone word 'groan' which appears twice in the square brackets, and which heightens the absurdity of Tom's melodramatic display.[2]

This is a slightly different question to any we have seen before. Instead of asking about the use of language, the paper is asking us to comment on the author's formatting choice.

Although less common, these sorts of questions do appear from time to time in 10+ papers – you might perhaps be asked why an author decided to put a paragraph break where they have, or why the author has used a particular piece of punctuation.

The trick is to look at the choice the author has made and to ask yourself what effect it has on you, the reader, and the reading experience.

What can be instructive here is to look at what the author might have done instead.

So let's look at the instance of square brackets at line 38:

"'I forgive you everything, Sid. [Groan.] Everything you've ever done to me.'

Instead, the author could have closed the speech marks midway through, and described who was groaning in a more conventional way, like this:

"I forgive you everything, Sid,' Tom said, with a groan. 'Everything you've ever done to me.'

This second version, however, has a different impact on us. It momentarily takes us out of the dialogue, and slows down our experience of the conversation. We might argue that it distracts from the dialogue, and thus disrupts its flow. Indeed, this is the argument I've made in my model answer. I point out that it allows the author to still add a detail that heightens the melodrama, while still keeping us engrossed in the dialogue.

Another word I might have used to make this argument is 'timing': the author uses the square brackets to sharpen the timing of the passage, so that its delivered to the reader faster, and arguably in a more entertaining way.

But as ever, it is important to acknowledge that there are other arguments that a candidate might have made that would have also won the marks. For instance, they could have argued that putting the 'groan' in square brackets within the dialogue, the author was emphasizing that the groan was not merely just a groan, but an integral part of the message he was trying to communicate; that the groan was in a way synonymous with the dialogue.[3]

The examiner will award one mark for a compelling and credible argument for why the author has used the square brackets and the impact it has on the reader – and a second mark for explaining the argument coherently and well.

6. The following words are underlined in the passage. Suggest another word or phrase to explain the meaning of each one, as it is used in the passage. [6]

a) Odious

Another word for 'odious' would be 'loathsome'.

b) Exertions

Another word for 'exertions' would be 'efforts'.

c) Joggle

Another word for 'joggle' would be 'shake'.

d) Genuine

Another word for 'genuine' would be 'sincere'.

e) Restored

Another word for 'restored' would be 'cured'.

7. Why does Tom's Aunt both laugh and cry at the end of the passage? [4]

Aunt Polly ends up both laughing and crying at the end of the passage because she has experienced a conflicting set of extreme emotions. On one hand, despite telling Sid she does not 'believe' that Tom is dying, Aunt Polly clearly experiences fear while responding to Sid's panic and Tom's play-acting – so much so that she 'her face grew white... and her lip trembled'. On the other hand, shortly after this, Tom tells her that his toe is 'mortified', an absurd claim which Polly finds extremely funny, and which immediately informs her that Tom is feigning. Polly's tears, then, appear to be tears of relief (there is, after all, no danger), whereas her laughter is a response to the ridiculousness of Tom's complaint.

The first mark here is for acknowledging that the reason Polly both laughed and cried at once was as a result of contradictory / conflicting emotions – the fact she was both fearful and amused.

The next mark is for explaining why Aunt Polly had been scared in the first place – that is, because Sid had convinced her that Tom was sick – as well as how we know that Polly was scared.

The third mark is for explaining why Aunt Polly, on encountering Tom, found herself highly entertained and amused (it is because Tom's melodramatic display was so obviously preposterous).

The fourth and final mark is for coherently bringing all of these ideas together: we want to acknowledge that her tears are a result of her fear, and her laughter the result of her being amused by Tom's melodrama.

8. Think about the passage as a whole. How does the author make the passage comical for the reader? [6]

Think about how Tom behaves, how Sid and his Aunt react, and our feelings about the various characters. Use your own words but also refer to evidence in the passage to support what you say.

The author generates comedy at the start of the passage by giving the reader an insight into Tom's mental processes. What stands out is the concept that Tom 'wished he was sick' so that 'he could stay home from school'. This is darkly humorous observational comedy, drawing attention to a human tendency to wish ill upon oneself in order to avoid a perceived greater ill. The comedy is enhanced further when Tom rules out complaining that 'one of his upper front teeth was loose' as his aunt was likely to 'pull it out'. This comically suggests there is a hierarchy of unpleasantness that Tom is attempting to navigate.[4] The author also creates comedy with the notion that Tom 'investigated his system' for illness: whereas sickness usually makes itself known against one's will, Tom is perversely trying to seek it out.

As the passage progresses, the author develops this comic conceit by having Tom start to believe his own absurd play-acting: we are told he 'fancied that he began to feel pain in the toe', and, later, that he 'was suffering in reality'. Again, this is observational comedy: the author is meditating on an absurd human tendency to believe one's own lies.

The author also injects comedy through the interactions between Tom and Sid. Tom's plan hinges on Sid buying into his play-acting; but Sid at first comically sleeps through Tom's groans ('Sid snored on') – the comedy is sharpened by Tom's protracted efforts, and Sid's stubborn refusal to wake.[5] That the supposedly sickly Tom is forced to display his abundant strength to shake Sid awake adds a layer of comic irony to the proceedings. The ensuing conversation adds a new comic dimension. Instead of merely pretending to be sick, Tom opts for absurd melodrama, and behaves as though he is dying: he displays the magnanimity of a man on his death-bed – 'I forgive everybody, Sid' – and offers up a will of absurdly modest items: 'give my window-sash and my cat with one eye to that new girl'.[6]

Physical comedy is achieved through the image of Aunt Polly '[flying] upstairs' with 'Sid and cousin Mary at her heels'. The wording implies a seriousness and panic, which the reader understands to be comically misplaced. The absurd and anticlimactic moment at which Tom proclaims his ailment – 'my sore toe's mortified' – deflates Aunt Polly's seriousness so rapidly, that she too is reduced to laughter at the absurdity of Tom's behaviour.

As at the end of the previous paper, we are presented with an essay style question. However, *this* final question is clearly worth more marks than the questions that preceded it within the paper – thereby indicating that the examiner wants a meatier, essay-style answer.

Again, the approach I suggest is a thematic one. Here is the very brief plan I put together before I started writing:

- Theme/Paragraph One: Tom's process of 'discovering' an illness. The concept itself – that one would wish to be sick – is absurd.
- Theme/Paragraph Two: The absurdity of Tom starting to believe his own lie.
- Theme/Paragraph Three: The comic interactions between Sid and Tom: Sid not waking up at first / Tom's melodramatic comments.
- Theme/Paragraph Four: The comic juxtaposition between Aunt Polly's dramatic response, and the anti-climax created by Tom's exposition.[7]

Given that the question is worth 6 marks, I knew I wanted at least three strong themes; however, I also knew that my second theme was quite brief, so I decided to have a fourth just to ensure that the examiner had no excuse to dock me marks.

The key thing is that, for each argument you make, you need to back it up with quotes from the passage that support your argument. Then you need to spend time analysing the quotes you put forward, looking at the effect they have on us as readers. If you can follow this recipe – thematic paragraphs, quotes to support your arguments, analysis of these quotes – you will be well on your way to scoring highly!

---

1. Faux is another word for fake!
2. To be melodramatic is to be overdramatic. Another good word with a similar meaning is 'histrionic'.
3. A synonym is a word with a similar meaning to another word. As a result, you'll be unsurprised to learn that if one thing is 'synonymous' to another thing, it means that they are alike!
4. A hierarchy refers to a system in which various things or people are ranked or ordered.
5. If something is protracted, it means it is drawn out over a substantial period of time.
6. We use the word magnanimity to describe behaviour that is exceptionally noble or high-minded.
7. Juxtaposition is when you contrast two very different things, and, through this comparison, draw attention to their differences.
    Exposition refers to text that explains a situation or set of circumstances to someone.

Paper Four: The Flying Blind Paper

This paper tests many of the same skills that the three previous papers have done. The key difference is that in The Flying Blind Paper, we are not told how many marks each question is worth! This can be incredibly frustrating, but it is nevertheless something you see from time to time in 10+ papers – and it means that we have to use our knowledge of 10+ papers in general to intuit what sort of answers the examiners are looking for. Let's dive on in!

The Tiredness of Rosabel
THE FLYING BLIND PAPER; 30 MINUTES

This extract is taken from a short story, and is set in early twentieth century London.

1   Rosabel was more than glad to reach Richmond Road, but from the corner of the street until she came to No. 26 she thought of those four flights of stairs up to her room. Oh, why four flights! It was really criminal to expect people to live so high up. Every house ought to have a lift, something simple and inexpensive, or else an electric
5   staircase like the one at Earl's Court—but four flights! When she stood in the hall and saw the first flight ahead of her and the stuffed albatross head on the landing, glimmering ghost-like in the light of the little gas jet, she almost cried. Well, they had to be faced; it was very like bicycling up a steep hill, but there was not the satisfaction of flying down the other side…

10 Her own room at last! She lit the gas, took off her hat and coat, skirt, blouse, unhooked her old flannel dressing-gown from behind the door, pulled it on, then unlaced her boots—on consideration her stockings were not wet enough to change.

It was just seven o'clock. If she pulled the blind up and put out the gas it was much more restful—Rosabel did not want to read. So she knelt down on the floor, pillowing
15 her arms on the window-sill … just one little sheet of glass between her and the great wet world outside!

Rosabel began to think of all that had happened during the day. Would she ever forget that awful woman in the grey mackintosh, or the girl who had tried on every hat in the shop?

20 But there had been one other—a girl with beautiful red hair and a white skin and eyes the colour of that green ribbon shot with gold they had got from Paris last week. Rosabel had seen her car at the door; a man had come in with her, quite a young man, and so well dressed.

"What is it exactly that I want, Harry?" she had said, as Rosabel gave her a hand-
25 mirror.

"You must have a black hat," he had answered, "a black hat with a feather that goes right round it and then round your neck and ties in a bow under your chin, and the ends tuck into your belt—a decent-sized feather."

The girl glanced at Rosabel laughingly. "Have you any hats like that?"

30 They had been very hard to please; Harry would demand the impossible, and Rosabel was almost in despair. Then she remembered the big, untouched box upstairs.

"Oh, one moment, Madam," she had said. "I think perhaps I can show you something that will please you better." She had run up, breathlessly, cut the cords, scattered
35 the tissue paper, and yes, there was the very hat—rather large, soft, with a great, curled feather, and a black velvet rose, nothing else. They had been charmed. The girl had put it on and then handed it to Rosabel.

"Let me see how it looks on you," she said, frowning a little, very serious indeed. Rosabel turned to the mirror and placed it on her brown hair, then faced them.

40 "Oh, Harry, isn't it adorable," the girl cried, "I must have that!" She smiled again at Rosabel. "It suits you, beautifully."

A sudden, ridiculous feeling of anger had seized Rosabel. She longed to throw the lovely, perishable thing in the girl's face, and bent over the hat, flushing.

"It's exquisitely finished off inside, Madam," she said. The girl swept out to her car,
45 and left Harry to pay and bring the box with him.

"I shall go straight home and put it on before I come out to lunch with you," Rosabel heard her say.

The man leant over her as she made out the bill, then, as he counted the money into her hand—"Ever been painted?" he said.

50 "No," said Rosabel, shortly, realising the swift change in his voice, the slight tinge of insolence, of familiarity.

"Oh, well you ought to be," said Harry. "You've got such a damned pretty little figure."

55 Rosabel did not pay the slightest attention. How handsome he had been! She had thought of no one else all day; his face fascinated her; she could see clearly his fine, straight eyebrows, and his hair grew back from his forehead with just the slightest suspicion of crisp curl, his laughing, disdainful mouth.

An extract adapted from Katherine Mansfield's The Tiredness of Rosabel

---

1. At the start of the passage, Rosabel enters her room. Name two things from paragraph two that Rosabel does once she enters her room.

2. Give two details from paragraph five that suggest that the female customer was visually attractive.

3. Look at lines 48 to 57. Give two details from this passage which suggest that Rosabel feels that Harry is a disrespectful individual.

4. Look at lines 30 to 37. Choose two phrases used by the writer which suggest that the two customers put Rosabel under pressure.

5. Explain how each of these phrases helps to convey the extent to which Rosabel was put under pressure.

6. Explain, using your own words, Rosabel's reaction to the woman's comment that the hat suited Rosabel beautifully (line 41)

7. Explain, using your own words, what the writer means by:

   a) Pillowing (line 14)

   b) Charmed (line 36)

   c) Seized (line 42)

   d) Exquisitely (line 44)

   e) Swift (line 50)

8. Re-read the opening paragraph. Explain how Rosabel feels as she prepares to mount the stairs. You should use details from the passage to support your answer.

Model Answers & Guidance

<u>1. At the start of the passage, Rosabel enters her room. Name two things from paragraph two that Rosabel does once she enters her room.</u>

Once Rosabel enters her room, she lit the gas and took off various articles of clothing, including her hat, coat, skirt and blouse.

This question can feel frustrating – if only because Rosabel takes off a number of items of clothing, and candidates might reasonably argue that each time she takes off another article, she is in a sense 'doing' something new.

However, my advice is to go above and beyond. We can see that Rosabel does more than just disrobe; she also lights the gas, unhooks her dressing gown, and puts her dressing gown on, and so forth.

Yes, a generous examiner might give you the marks if you were to write that two things Rosabel does upon getting inside are: a) take off her hat; and b) take off her coat. But a stricter examiner may take the view that taking off one's clothes should count as just one action, and thus we are safer to think of disrobing as one action, and then to name one of the other actions as well (such as lighting the gas, or putting on the dressing gown).[1]

Remember, we don't merely want to do the bare minimum. We want to make sure that the examiner has no excuse to dock us marks.

As mentioned already, we are not being told how many marks are at stake for any of the questions in this paper. However, by clumping together the act of 'taking off various articles of clothing', and *then* naming a second action, I can feel confident I am scoring full marks.

2. Give two details from paragraph five that suggest that the female customer was visually attractive.

> **One indication that the female customer was visually attractive is the description of her hair, which is described as 'beautiful red hair'. The word 'beautiful' fairly explicitly nods to the aesthetically pleasing nature of the woman's hair – the word is a synonym for 'visually attractive'.[2] Another indication the customer was attractive is the description of her eye colour, which is likened to 'green ribbon shot with gold' that had been sourced from 'Paris.' Ribbon is a luxurious material, known for its vibrant colours, which suggests the woman's eyes, too, are vibrant and luxurious-seeming; moreover, the idea that her eyes are 'shot with gold' – a colour synonymous with beauty – further creates a sense that this woman's eyes are visually appealing.**

We are being asked here for two details that suggest that the female customer was visually attractive. However, because we are not being told how many marks are at stake, we might feel uncertain whether to simply list two details – or whether to expand on *how* each of the details tell us that the female customer was visually attractive.

My advice in a paper like this is to take the more rigorous approach. We first want to pick out two details (and use quotations from the text to do so); and then we want to briefly discuss how these details/quotations work to portray the female customer as visually attractive.

The first detail I seize on is the description of the woman's hair, which is described as 'beautiful red hair'. This quote does not require too much analysis, since it very clearly says that the woman's hair was 'beautiful' – a synonym for visually attractive.

The second detail I pick out in my answer is the way her eyes are likened to 'green ribbon shot with gold'. This quote does require a bit more explanation as to how it presents the female customer as beautiful, since it is a little less obvious – and I focus in on both the way that ribbon is usually associated with luxury decorations, and how gold is considered decorative and beautiful. In truth, if I had focused on how just the ribbon or just the gold conveys the customer's beauty, I would likely have done enough. However, I decided to cover both in order to really dazzle the examiner!

3. Look at lines 48 to 57. Give two details from this passage which suggest that Rosabel feels that Harry is a disrespectful individual.

One detail that suggests Rosabel feels that Harry is disrespectful is the way she detects a 'slight twinge of insolence' when he asks whether Rosabel had ever been painted. The word 'insolence' implies a degree of audacity, of overstepping the bounds of decorum.[3] A second detail that points to Harry's air of disrespect is his 'laughing, disdainful mouth': this – in particular the word 'disdainful' – hints that his manner was supercilious and perhaps even impolite towards Rosabel.

This question very closely resembles the one immediately beforehand. As such, we want to employ similar tactics: we want to pick out two details that suggest Rosabel feels that Harry is disrespectful, and use short quotes from the passage in the process of doing so; and then we want to explain how the detail/quote we have extracted portrays Harry as disrespectful.

The first detail I pick out is the 'twinge of insolence' that Rosabel detects in Harry's voice; and, to give the examiner no excuse to dock me marks, I then dissect the word 'insolence' – the fact it implies that Harry is overstepping acceptable codes of conduct, and thus points to a disrespectful strain in his character.

I then follow the almost identical rubric with the second detail I pick out: the fact that Harry is described as having a 'laughing, disdainful mouth.' In this quote, it is important in particular to spend time focusing on the words 'disdainful', which implies Harry is haughty and arrogant in his dealings with Rosabel.

It is important to note at this point, however, that there are other details a student might pick out that – if adequately analysed – could still score them the marks.

One such detail is the way Harry 'leant over [Rosabel] as she made out the bill', and continued to do so while paying her. If a candidate capably argues that Harry's disregard for Rosabel's personal space points to his disrespectful character, they would likely score the marks.

Another detail a student might seize upon is the way in which Harry's voice is also described as having a twinge of 'familiarity'. This is a more subtle detail to run with, but a candidate would score marks if they observed that it is inappropriate for Harry to have a tone of familiarity with a stranger – and that it suggests he was disrespectfully overstepping.

4. Look at lines 30 to 37. Choose two phrases used by the writer which suggest that the two customers put Rosabel under pressure.

> **Two phrases that suggests that the two customers put Rosabel under pressure include the comment that 'Harry would demand the impossible', but also the observation that 'She [Rosabel] had run up, breathlessly'.**

This question is slightly different in its formulation to the previous two: it asks for two 'phrases' instead of two 'details'. And given that the very next question asks us to 'explain' the phrases we are picking out in question four, we know that all we need to do here is pick out two short quotations that suggest that customers put Rosabel under pressure, since we'll be doing the explaining in question five.

The two quotes I've picked out are likely the most obvious ones; though others phrases that would also score marks here include 'They had been very hard to please' and 'Rosabel was almost in despair'.

<u>5. Explain how each of these phrases helps to convey the extent to which Rosabel was put under pressure.</u>

> **The idea that 'Harry would demand the impossible' of Rosabel fairly explicitly emphasises how he put her under pressure – the idea that Harry would 'demand' suggests that he was firing imperious orders (as opposed to mere requests) at Rosabel, orders she was being uncomfortably compelled to follow. Moreover, the hyperbolic notion that he was asking her to carry out 'the impossible' draws attention to the strenuousness of his requests.[4]**
>
> **That Rosabel 'had run up, breathlessly' in search of the hat illustrates how she was put under pressure in a different way – namely, by drawing attention the physical strain the couple's requests had put her under. Rosabel is working in a clothing store; yet the couple has put Rosabel under such pressure that she is nevertheless being required to exert herself in an extremely physical way, hence her breathlessness.**

Because this question – unlike questions two and three – is explicitly asking us to engage in analysis of quotations, we want our explanation to be a little bit more detailed.

Notice how I analyse two different elements of the first quotation I've chosen: both the word 'demand' – which suggests that the couple were firing orders at Rosabel – and the notion of them asking 'the impossible', and the way this uses exaggeration to further underscore the pressure Rosabel was under. Since I had something insightful to say about two different elements of the phrase, I decided to go to town and analyse both; after all, we have not been told how many marks are at stake, and I want to ensure that I'm not falling short.

The second quotation I've picked is different insofar as it is more implicit (as opposed to explicit) in its portrayal of Rosabel as under pressure. All the same, I make sure to discuss how the author uses Rosabel's strained physical state as a means to nod to the pressure she is under – and I placed the idea of her being breathless under particular scrutiny.

If a candidate had chosen the quote 'They had been very hard to please' as one of their two phrases, they would have needed to have honed in on the idea of the couple being 'hard to please', and the way this implies that Rosabel – prior to eventually finding the right hat – had likely tried and failed to meet their high expectations.

Alternatively, if a candidate had chosen the phrase 'Rosabel was almost in despair', they would again need to focus on how the author uses Rosabel's distress – this time emotional as opposed to physical – to indirectly point towards the pressure the couple placed her under, as well as the extreme emotional state conjured up by the word 'despair'.

Candidates whose answers here are too brief do risk losing marks – even if they have picked strong quotes.

6. Explain, using your own words, Rosabel's reaction to the woman's comment that the hat suited Rosabel beautifully (line 41)

> **When the woman observes that the hat suited Rosabel beautifully, Rosabel experiences an intense feeling of resentment. By having had Rosabel try on the hat, the woman (whether intentionally or not) taunts Rosabel with a luxury item that she was unable to afford for herself. As a result, Rosabel feels a spike of frustration so intense that she momentarily longs to throw the hat in the woman's face. This feeling also elicits in Rosabel a physical reaction (she flushes), though she attempts to conceal this by bowing her head.**

By this point, candidates should be getting used to questions that ask them to use their own words. The key is to try and rephrase things using vocabulary that largely differs from the vocabulary the author uses.

With regards to this particular question, the examiner is looking for candidates to both: a) explain the nature of Rosabel's reaction to the comment – namely, she reacts with resentment, which causes her to flush, and which she tried to hide; and b) explain why the comment elicits such resentment in Rosabel – namely, because she is unable to afford an item of such luxury as this hat, and feels as though, by having her try it on, the woman has been taunting her.

Candidates must explain both of these dimensions in order to score full marks. If they tackle just one of these two lines of thought, they are likely to cap themselves at half marks.

7. Explain, using your own words, what the writer means by:

a) Pillowing (line 14)

> **Pillowing, as used in the extract, seems to mean to lay something down in such a way that it seems to assume the shape of a pillow; but it also potentially implies that this something – in this case, Rosabel's arms – is in fact being used as a surface to rest one's head.**

b) Charmed (line 36)

> **Charmed, as used in the extract, means enticed and pleased.**

c) Seized (line 42)

> **Seized, as used in the extract, means grabbed or suddenly overcome.**

d) Exquisitely (line 44)

> **Exquisitely, as used in the extract, means beautifully or attractively.**

e) Swift (line 50)

> **Swift, as used in the extract, means rapid or quick.**

This definition-style question is, by and large, similar to the other definition-style questions we have encountered already: our best approach is to offer similar words that we could comfortably swap in for the words we are being asked to define.

However, there is one word here – pillowing – that is a bit more complicated, since its meaning is not straightforward. Let's take a look at the sentence in which the word appears:

'So she knelt down on the floor, pillowing her arms on the window-sill'

It would appear that it is Rosabel's arms that are doing the 'pillowing.' However, it is unclear whether this means that she is placing them on the window sill in a way that makes them almost look like a pillow – or whether she is actually using them as a surface on which to rest her head.

Candidates who offer just one of these interpretations are still likely to score a mark. However, the examiner understands that the word is ambiguous, and they are hoping to see candidates explore this ambiguity and discuss the two different potential meanings – and those that do so successfully will likely score a bonus mark.

8. Re-read the opening paragraph. Explain how Rosabel feels as she prepares to mount the stairs. You should use details from the passage to support your answer.

The overarching emotion Rosabel feels as she prepares to mount the stairs is resentment – not only towards the ordeal ahead, but also the way in which the world is ordered in general. The free indirect narration gives us an explicit insight into Rosabel's mindset: namely, that she believed 'it was really criminal to expect people to live so high up'.[5] Encoded in this mentality is not only a resentment at having to climb the stairs, but also anger at an economic set-up that finds its permissible to foist this ordeal on those with limited means. This streak of resentment, however, is emphasized time and again: it is apparent in the reforms Rosabel thinks ought to be implemented – 'every house ought to have a lift' – but also more subtly through the use of punctuation, such as the exclamation mark after the phrase 'but four flights.'

As Rosabel actually reaches the bottom of the stairs 'and saw the first flight ahead', she also exhibits another emotion – namely, that of being almost entirely overwhelmed – which is neatly captured in the succinct phrase that 'she almost cried'. This powerful emotion, though, is counterbalanced by a sense of almost stoic resignation that Rosabel is able to conjure up in the next moment, and which is captured with the sentiment that 'they had to be faced'.[6]

Interestingly, however, the paragraph's final sentence in fact circles back to reiterating Rosabel's sense of resentment. In it, Rosabel likens the ordeal to 'bicycling up a steep hill', but bitterly meditates on the comparative lack of reward at the end of the exertion: 'but there was not the satisfaction of flying down the other side'. Rosabel, in short, resentfully feels as though the stairs represent exertion without reward.

Although this question is not asking us to comment on the passage as a whole, there is still a strong clue that the examiner is hoping to see an essay-style response – namely, the request that we 'use details from the passage to support [our] answer.' This implies that the examiner wants to see us quoting repeatedly from the passage, and offering up analysis of these quotes.

Moreover, the fact this is the final question in the paper also hints that the examiner is looking for a longer response, since these essay-style questions virtually always appear at the end of 10+ papers.

Before launching into my response, I put together a very brief thematic plan:

- Resentment towards both the stairs and the world at large
- Overwhelmed yet paradoxically stoic.
- Resentment re-emerging

As mentioned before, I believe that taking a quick moment to plan is advantageous, as it means we have rubric to follow once we start composing our response. And as you can see, although my plan is brief, I'm trying to grapple with the nuances of Rosabel's emotions.

Since this essay is only asking us to comment on a single paragraph within the passage, it is likely to be a little bit shorter than some of the essay-style responses we see in 10+ papers. Nevertheless, the examiner is still looking for at the very least two or three substantial paragraphs. A candidate would still pick up marks if they made just one substantial argument – for instance, if they only focused on Rosabel's resentment. However, they would certainly be missing out on further marks if the scope of their argument did not go beyond this.

---

1. Disrobing is a fancy word for taking off one's clothes!
2. The word aesthetic basically refers to how things look. To be aesthetically pleasing, then, is to be visually attractive.
3. Acting with decorum basically means to act politely and with appreciation for social rules and niceties. Therefore, to overstep the bounds of decorum is to flout social rules and niceties.
4. If someone is speaking hyperbolically, it means they are using lots of exaggeration. So something that is hyperbolic is something that has been greatly exaggerated.
5. I know 'free indirect narration' sounds like an intimidatingly technical phrase, but let me explain.
    You may already know that a first person story is one written from a character's own point of view ('I went there. I did this'), and that a third person story is one in which a narrator describes the actions of the story's character's ('He did this. She did that'). But have you ever noticed how, when you are reading a third person story, it sometimes still feels as if you are subtly getting a certain character's distinct point of view? As if the narrator perhaps has a secret insight into that character's mind? Well, this is known as the 'free indirect third person;' and, while technically still a type of third person narration, it feels a bit like a blend between first person and third person.
    Examiners like it when you have sophisticated technical vocabulary up your sleeve. I want you to be able to spot it when you see it, as I have done here.
6. To be stoic is to be unemotional in the face of circumstances that would ordinarily induce extreme emotions. It's a bit like having a stiff upper lip!

Paper Five: The Reasoning & Reading Between the Lines Paper

Although a number of the questions in this paper are similar to questions we've encountered already, they are, by and large, more difficult. We will encounter retrieval questions that exercise our reasoning skills to a greater degree; and we will encounter questions that require us to make trickier inferences than we have hitherto been required to make. To score the marks here, we will need to be accomplished at the art of "reading between the lines" – that is, understanding what the text is saying implicitly as opposed to explicitly. Good luck!

Meteor Men of Mars
THE REASONING & READING BETWEEN THE
LINES PAPER; 30 MINUTES

This extract is taken from near the start of a short story, and explores an incident experienced by two men who are fishing out at sea.

---

1   The sun was a huge red ball balanced on the rim of the sea when Frank suddenly felt a jerk on his fishing line that nearly wrenched his arm from its socket. He said nothing. His lips merely tightened, eagerly, as he wished to surprise his companion by hauling in the big one unexpectedly.

5   But this proved harder than he thought.

His potential catch darted off with such a burst of speed and strength that it dragged boat, anchor and all!

"Hey!" yelled Storm, clutching the boat sides to hold himself. "What's on that jig? A shark? Better cut that line before it swamps us!"

10 "Like heck I will!" Hammond grunted, hanging on to the line with both taped hands. "This must be the grandfather of all big blues. That new hat's in the bag!"

With both feet braced against the thwarts, he leaned back and pulled with all his strength. Bit by bit he hauled the "big one" in close, till finally he was able to lift it out of the water and into the boat.

15 Both men exclaimed in amazement at the thing which came over the side and clanked to the bottom of the boat. It was neither a giant bluefish nor a shark. It was a

shiny, iridescent object, slightly shaped like a shark, but still now, and seemingly lifeless.

"What kind of a fish do you call that?" asked Storm disgustedly, leaning forward for better view of the catch. "It looks like a cross between a shark and a toy submarine."

"Damned if it don't!" Hammond replied, staring bewilderedly at his catch.

The thing was about thirty inches in length, with both vertical and dorsal fins. But instead of one dorsal fin it was equipped with four fins placed equidistantly around the body. These fins contained numerous tubular quills or spines with round openings at the ends, and Hammond's hook had caught between two of these spines. It was as heavy as if made of steel, but despite its weight and metallic sound when struck, it appeared to be constructed entirely of a bluish, iridescent mother-of-pearl.

Hammond removed his hook from between the spines, and lifted his catch onto the empty boat seat between them.

"Better heave it overboard," advised Storm, seriously. "It might be a new-fangled type of mine or bomb. I don't like the looks—"

He stood, open-mouthed, as the "thing" suddenly shot off the boat seat with a hissing roar like that of a small rocket. It scorched the paint as it took off with small, orange-green flares emanating from the tubular quills. It shot upward with incredible speed and was almost immediately lost to view.

Storm's mouth closed slowly. "Hell!" he said, a little dazedly. "I'm afraid to start fishing again, Frank. Might catch a cross between a battleship and a whale."

"I'm hauling up anchor," Hammond countered, grimly. "I don't like the looks of this at all. Let's call it a night. The coast guard ought to hear of this."

He got one hand on the anchor rope and was starting to hoist in when the strange "catch" suddenly reappeared. It came down in a long slant, circled over the skiff a few times, and finally settled on the scorched seat from which it had taken off.

Hammond stared at the thing and swore. Peter Storm took a firm hold of his oar.

Holes suddenly appeared in the strange craft. Hammond noticed that there were no doors in evidence. The holes seemed to dilate open, like camera shutters, in the gleaming body.

From these openings a host of small creatures crawled. They swarmed out toward both ends of the boat seat.

Storm straightened, oar in hand. "Ants!" he snapped, disgustedly. He began to swing the ash blade down on the scurrying creatures.

The things continued to move about, apparently unharmed. Dents appeared in the oar and in the seat.

Hammond bent over the scurrying creatures and studied them. "No use, Pete," he muttered. "They're not ants. There's no division of head, thorax and abdomen.
55 They're eight-legged —more like spiders." His startled surprise was fading under the prod of scientific curiosity. "Funny thing, Pete—the legs and shells seem to be composed of the same substance as the 'thing' they come from. Look!"

Storm dropped his oar and came forward.

An extract adapted from The Meteor Men of Mars, by Harry Cord and Otis Adelbert Kline

---

1. At what time of day did the events described take place? How can you tell? [2].

2. Why does Frank Hammond choose not say anything when he first felt a jerk on his fishing line? [2]

3. What is Storm's full name, and why does he say that Hammond should cut his fishing line? [2]

4. Using facts from the whole story, explain how we can tell that these two men had been fishing before. Quote some phrases from the story which suggest this. [4]

5. After removing his hook from the object he caught, where does Frank Hammond place the object? [1]

6. Why did Storm take 'a firm hold of his oar'? (line 43) [2]

7. Explain fully and in your own words why Frank Hammond's 'startled surprise' began to fade (line 55) [4]

8. Why did Storm drop his oar at the end of the story? (line 58) [2]

9. Look at lines 15 to 58.

What are Storm and Hammond's feelings about the object they discover? (You should discuss at least 3 different moments). [6]

Model Answers & Guidance

<u>1. At what time of day did the events described take place? How can you tell? [2].</u>

> **The events described in the passage take place at sunset. The first clue is contained within the opening sentence, which makes clear that the sun was on the edge of the horizon – 'the sun... balanced on the rim of the sea' – suggesting it is either sunrise or sunset. Later in the passage the reader is given greater clarity when Hammond says 'let's call it a night', indicating that it must be sunset, *not* sunrise.**

Although at first glance this appears to be a retrieval question, we are in fact being asked to engage our reasoning skills, too.

Most students will be able to infer from the opening sentence – 'The sun was a huge red ball balanced on the rim of the sea' – that this passage is set at either sunrise or sunset. However, it requires a keener eye to spot the detail at line 39, where Hammond says 'let's call it a night'. This expression – which means something to the effect of 'let's stop for the night' – indicates that it is evening as opposed to morning.

To score both marks, the examiner will want the candidate to invoke *both* of these pieces of information and to thus conclude that the events take place at sunset.

If a candidate just invokes the second detail, and asserts that the events take place 'night', they are likely to score just one mark.

Moreover, if the candidate invokes just the opening sentence, and correctly guesses that the events take place at sunset, they will also be capped at just one mark.

2. Why does Frank Hammond choose not say anything when he first felt a jerk on his fishing line? [2]

> **Frank Hamond chose not to say anything when he felt a jerk on his line because he had not wanted to alert his friend to the fact that he was on the brink of catching something. Instead, given that the strong tug on the line implied that he might have snagged a very large fish, Hammond had wanted to surprise his friend by suddenly producing an impressive catch.**

The first mark here is for acknowledging that Hammond chose to say silent when he first felt a jerk on his fishing line because he did not want his friend to realise that he had hooked something substantial.

The second mark is for explaining *why* Hammond did not want Storm to realise there was something at the end of the line: namely, because he wanted to surprise Storm by suddenly pulling in a really impressive catch.

3. What is Storm's full name, and why does he say that Hammond should cut his fishing line? [2]

> **Storm's full name is Peter Storm. Storm tells Hammond to cut his fishing line because he fears that the force being exerted on Hammond's line is so great that it might cause their boat to capsize, thereby 'swamp[ing]' them.**

The first mark is simply for correctly identifying Storm's first name as Peter. This is revealed at line 43: 'Peter Storm took a firm hold of his oar.'

The second mark is for explaining why Storm tells Hammond to cut the line. A candidate will not get the mark if they simply say that Storm tells Hammond to cut the line because he fears that the entity at the end of the line will 'swamp' them. Rather, to get the mark, the candidate must show that they understand what this expression means: namely, that Storm is worried that if Hammond does not cut the line, the boat may capsize.

4. Using facts from the whole story, explain how we can tell that these two men had been fishing before. Quote some phrases from the story which suggest this. [4]

One key clue that Storm and Hammond had been fishing before is their use of technical and colloquial language associated with the activity.[1] Early on, Storm asks 'what's on that jig?' – the word 'jig' clearly a technical term for an element on the fishing rod – then uses the expression 'swamps us', the sort of slang one would expect from someone accustomed to boating. In response, Hammond speculates that he has caught the 'grandfather of all big blues' – his use of colloquial language ('big blue') also suggests that he is well acquainted with the world of fishing.[2] Later, Hammond again uses a colloquial sea-faring expression that suggests he has likely been on a fishing boat before: 'I'm hauling up anchor'.

Another clue that the pair have been fishing before is the way they physically demonstrate their familiarity with boating and fishing equipment. Hammond is able to keep hold of the fishing line despite a force that nearly 'wrenched his arm from its socket', implying a dexterity with the equipment; he knows to tug the line with his 'feet braced against the thwarts'; he wears fishing tape on his hands ('taped hands') which suggests a professionalism; and, a little later, Hammond hoists the 'anchor rope' with just one hand.

Here we have a style of question we have not yet encountered in this guide. Basically, it presents the student with an inference from the passage (in this case, that the men had been fishing before) and it asks the student to not only pick out details that support this inference, but also to explain how these details do so.

A key detail to pick up is the language the men use: more specifically, the fact they use technical language that suggests a familiarity with fishing and boating, as well as slang terms that also suggest they are steeped in this world. One mark is available for making this observation. The second mark is for picking out at least two good quotes from the passage that illustrate this point, and offering coherent analysis of these quote.

The second detail the candidate needs to identify is the men's comfort with the fishing apparatus: more specifically, Hammond's ability to wield the fishing rod, and his specialist equipment. Again, one mark is for making this point. Another is for extracting (and then briefly dissecting) at least two good quotes that support this point.

5. After removing his hook from the object he caught, where does Frank Hammond place the object? [1]

After removing the hook from the object, Hammond places it on the empty boat seat situated between him and Storm.

This is a straightforward retrieval question. The answer is at lines 28-29, where we learn that Hammond 'lifted his catch onto the empty boat seat between them.'

6. Why did Storm take 'a firm hold of his oar'? (line 43) [2]

Storm took 'a firm hold of his oar' because he was preparing to protect himself with it. The strange item had not only departed their boat with such force that it 'scorched the paint' on the seat, but it had also re-appeared with precision and intent, having 'circled over the skiff a few times'. Given these details, as well as the fact that Storm had already speculated it might be weapon – 'mine or bomb' – it is clear that Storm intended to use the oar as a protective weapon against the item.

Here we are being asked to read between the lines.

The first mark is for correctly stating that Storm took a firm hold of his oar because he was preparing to defend himself with it.

The second mark is for explaining how we know this. Above, I have explored the ways in which the text established to the reader (prior to Storm taking hold of the oar) that Storm considered the object a threat – something against which he felt he needed to protect himself.

Alternatively, a student might have instead focused on how Storm later used the oar as a weapon – 'He began to swing the ash blade down on the scurrying creatures' – and how, retrospectively, this informs us that Storm had taken 'a firm hold of his oar' at line 43 because he intended to use it to defend himself. This approach would also win the candidate the second mark.

7. Explain fully and in your own words why Frank Hammond's 'startled surprise' began to fade (line 55) [4]

> **Hammond's 'startled surprise' began to subside as a result of him becoming technically fascinated with the small creatures that had appeared from within the object.**
>
> **At first, when confronted with these creatures – which Storm initially identified as ants – both Hammond and Storm appeared to be in a state of shock. However, when Hammond drew closer to the creatures, he saw that they in fact lacked the physical attributes of ants. While this in itself ought to have been a surprising revelation – after all, it raised the possibility that this was a totally undocumented species – the process of examining the anatomy of the creatures paradoxically subdued Hammond's sense of surprise.³ Hammond instead found himself distracted (and his surprise displaced) by a scientific urge to mentally catalogue the specific attributes of these creatures.**

That this question is worth four marks indicates that we want to be putting forward a fairly meaty explanation here.

The first mark is for acknowledging the overarching reason why Hammond's startled surprise began to fade: namely, due to the potency of his technical fascination with the creatures.

The second and third marks can be won by giving a bit more detail as to how Hammond's technical fascination grew to eclipse his surprise: that is, the way in which he a) drew nearer, thereby allowing him to get a better view of these creatures; and b) found himself enticed by their anatomies.

The fourth mark is for coherency of the response / the candidate's ability to capably rephrase things in their own words.

8. Why did Storm drop his oar at the end of the story? (line 58) [2]

> **Storm dropped his oar at the end of the story in response to Hammond beckoning him over to scrutinise the creatures. It is likely that Hammond's calmer demeanour motivated Storm to give up his weapon – it made Storm feel less threatened – but also that Storm was distracted from the imperative to defend himself by Hammond's remarkable observations. One also imagines that Storm likely decided it would be cumbersome to inspect the creatures while grasping the oar, and thus dispensed of it.**

The reader is not explicitly told why Storm dropped his oar at the end of the story; rather, this is something the examiner is asking us to infer.

Let's look again at the lines in question:

> '[Hammond's] startled surprise was fading under the prod of scientific curiosity. "Funny thing, Pete—the legs and shells seem to be composed of the same substance as the 'thing' they come from. Look!"
>
> Storm dropped his oar and came forward.'

We can see that, just before Storm drops his oar, Hammond has become considerably calmer. And that Hammond, with the word 'Look', appears to be beckoning Storm over.

It is thus reasonable to infer that Storm jettisons the oar at least in part because Hammond's calm demeanour has made him feel less defensive – and in least in part because he wishes to inspect the creatures, which is either distracting him from the imperative to defend himself, and/or motivating him to lay the burdensome oar aside to get a better look.[4]

Another argument a candidate might make is that Storm lays the oar down because, when he strikes the creatures just a few lines earlier, the creatures come out unscathed: 'apparently unharmed'. As such, Storm arguably lays it down because he is beginning to realise that it does little good.

There are two marks up for grabs here. To score both, the candidate must make two credible arguments (each one worth a mark apiece).

9. Look at lines 15 to 58

What are Storm and Hammond's feelings about the object they discover? (You should discuss at least 3 different moments). [6]

Perhaps the most intense feeling induced in Storm and Hammond by the object is one of bewilderment. The reader learns that, on discovering the object, 'both [Storm and Hammond] exclaimed in amazement' – the word 'amazement' hinting at how the object confounded their comprehension – and the query Storm utters only furthers this impression: 'What kind of a fish do you call that?' Indeed, Storm's attempt moments later to categorise the object ('a cross between a shark and a toy submarine') only redoubles this sense of bewilderment: his urge to categorise tacitly acknowledges the degree to which the object bewilderingly defies categorisation.[5] Yet if the men are bewildered at first, they are all the more so as the object exhibits increasingly outlandish behaviour.[6] Storm

> is left 'open-mouthed' (body language synonymous with bewilderment) when the object launches off the seat, and, after the object lands, Hammond stares at it and swears, behaviour again suggestive of confoundment.
>
> Also evident in both men (and arguably a direct consequence of their bewilderment) is a sense of trepidation and caution towards the object. This is best exemplified when, just before the object shoots into the sky, Storm counsels that it is best to 'heave it overboard' because 'it might be a new-fangled type of mine or bomb'. That Storm's trepidation is shared by Hammond is confirmed when, after the object disappears into the sky, Hammond asserts that he 'don't like the looks of this at all' and that he believes they ought to warn the authorities ('coast guard ought to hear of this'). When Storm 'took a firm hold of his oar' after the object returns, this marks a heightening in his trepidation: he is preparing to defend himself against the object.
>
> Another feeling the object elicits in Storm in particular is disgust. This is explicitly alluded to as the object is brought on board: Storm comments on the object 'disgustedly'. Near the end of the passage, when creatures exit the object, we again see the word 'disgustedly' used to describe Storm's tone (this time as Storm mistakes the creatures for ants). Although the word is used to describe his reaction to the occupants of the object (and not the object itself), it nevertheless reinforces the sense that the object itself elicits profound disgust in Storm.

We are at the end of the paper, and we have a question that is not only worth more marks than the questions that came prior, but is asking us to comment on a large section of the passage, while also inviting us to discuss at least three discrete moments in the passage.

This should be starting to feel familiar – because yet again we have an essay-style question to finish off the paper.

True to form, I put together a quick plan before starting my response:

1. Bewilderment and confusion.
2. Trepidation and caution.
3. Disgust (particularly seen in Storm).

Since there are six marks at stake, I was working on the basis that each paragraph should be meaty enough to be worth two marks in its own right (though I knew that my opening paragraph was going to be especially meaty, and would hopefully be scoring me three marks off the bat, thereby giving me a nice cushion going forwards).

As an aside, do not be thrown off by the examiner's demand that we 'discuss at least 3 different moments'. This instruction is there for candidates who might not think things fully through and end up focusing on a very small piece of text. However, in my experience, if you employ a thematic approach, you will organically find yourself covering at least three moments in the text either way.

As ever, make sure that you are quoting regularly from the text, and that you are spending at least some time dissecting the quote and discussing how they advance your argument. This is, after all, an essential ingredient to any good essay-style response.

---

1. Colloquial language is language used in a specific community or among a specific group of people, and is more informal / conversational in nature.
2. To be acquainted with something is to be familiar with it.
3. An undocumented species is a species that has no record of ever having been encountered before.
4. To jettison something is to throw it away or dispose of it.
5. If something is tacit, it means that it is not said explicitly, but it is still something we can infer.
6. Something outlandish is something unusual and/or bizarre.

Paper Six: The Consider Deeply Paper

This paper is in many respects the hardest in the book, because it requires us to exercise not just our analytical powers, but also our creative and speculative powers. Yet while questions that stretch us creatively may present unique challenges, they also represent a unique chance to have some fun with the material, and to dazzle/impress the examiner in unexpected ways!

The Odour of Chrysanthemums

This passage is taken from the start of a short story set in Nottinghamshire, England, in the early twentieth century.

1   Workers, single, trailing and in groups, passed like shadows diverging home. Nearby, at the edge of the railway track, there stood a low cottage. A large bony vine clutched at the house, as if to claw down the tiled roof. Round the bricked yard grew a few wintry primroses. Beyond, the long, bush-covered garden sloped downwards. There
5   were some twiggy apple trees, winter-crack trees, and ragged cabbages. Beside the path hung dishevelled pink chrysanthemums*, like pink cloths hung on bushes. A woman came stooping out of the chicken coop, half-way down the garden. She closed and padlocked the door, then drew herself erect, having brushed some bits from her white apron.

10 She was a tall, handsome woman, with definite black eyebrows. Her smooth black hair was parted exactly. For a few moments she stood steadily watching the workers as they passed along the railway: then she turned in the direction of the brook beyond the garden. Her face was calm and set, her mouth was closed with disillusionment. After a moment she called:

15 "John!" There was no answer. She waited, and then said distinctly:

"Where are you?"

"Here!" replied a child's sulky voice from among the bushes. The woman looked piercingly through the dusk.

"Are you at that brook?" she asked sternly.

20 For answer the child showed himself before the raspberry-canes that rose like whips. He was a small, sturdy boy of five. He stood quite still, defiantly.

"Oh!" said the mother, conciliated. "I thought you were down at that wet brook—and you remember what I told you——"

The boy did not move or answer.

25 "Come, come on," she said more gently, "it's getting dark. There's your grandfather: he's driving the engine down the line now!"

The lad advanced slowly, with resentful, taciturn movement. He was dressed in trousers and waistcoat of cloth that was too thick and hard for the size of the garments. They were evidently cut down from a man's clothes.

30 As they went slowly towards the house he tore at the ragged wisps of chrysanthemums and dropped the petals in handfuls along the path.

"Don't do that—it does look nasty," said his mother. He refrained, and she, suddenly pitiful, broke off a twig with three or four wan flowers and held them against her face. When mother and son reached the yard her hand hesitated, and instead of
35 laying the flower aside, she pushed it in her apron-band. The mother and son stood at the foot of the three steps looking across railway tracks. The trundle of the small train was imminent.

Suddenly the engine loomed past the house and came to a stop opposite the gate.

The engine-driver, a short man with round grey beard, leaned out of the cab high
40 above the woman.

"Have you got a cup of tea?" he said in a cheery, hearty fashion.

* chrysanthemums: a type of flower.

An extract adapted from D H Lawrence's The Odour of Chrysanthemums

---

1. What is the name of the young boy in this extract? [1]

2. During what time of day does the story take place? [1]

3. How are the young boy and the train driver related? [1]

4. Explain the meaning of the following words in bold, as used in the passage: [3]

   a) 'her mouth was closed with **disillusionment**' (line 13)

   b) 'She waited, and then said **distinctly**' (line 15)

   c) **'The trundle of the small train was imminent'** (line 37)

5. The narrator describes the workers as passing 'like shadows diverging home' (line 1).

What does this simile tell you about the appearance of the workers? [2]

6 (a). 'Suddenly the engine loomed past the house and came to a stop opposite the gate.'

This sentence has been given a paragraph all to itself. Can you suggest why? [1]

6 (b). The story is written in the third person. Why do you think the writer chose to write in this way? (The third person is when a story is told by a narrator, and not by one of the characters in the story). [1]

7. What do you think will happen next? Explain your answer with reference to the passage as a whole. [4]

Q8 requires a longer, more detailed answer

8. The writer of the story makes frequent mentions of plants and flowers. In what ways does the passage use plants and flowers to create atmosphere? [6]

Refer to details in the text to back up your ideas.

You might write about:

- The plants and flowers described in the first paragraph
- The bush next to which the boy appears
- How the boy treats the chrysanthemums
- How the mother treats the chrysanthemums

Model Answers & Guidance

1. What is the name of the young boy in this extract? [1]

The young boy in this extract is called John.

The answer to this can be found at line 15, which reads as follows: '"John!" There was no answer.'

2. During what time of day does the story take place? [1]

The events in this story take place at dusk.

At lines 17 to 18 we learn that 'The woman looked piercingly through the dusk.' As such, we know that the story takes place at dusk.

3. How are the young boy and the train driver related? [1]

The train driver is the young boy's grandfather.

or…

The young boy is the train driver's grandson.

The answer to this retrieval question can be found in the woman's comments at lines 25-26, which reads as follows: 'There's your grandfather: he's driving the engine down the line now!"

4. Explain the meaning of the following words in bold, as used in the passage: [3]

a) 'her mouth was closed with **disillusionment**' (line 13)

The word disillusionment here means cynicism or an air of disappointment.

b) 'She waited, and then said **distinctly**' (line 15)

The word distinctly here means clearly.

c) '**The trundle of the small train was imminent**' (line 37)

The word imminent here means due to happen very soon.

5. The narrator describes the workers as passing 'like shadows diverging home' (line 1).

What does this simile tell you about the appearance of the workers? [2]

By describing the workers as passing 'like shadows diverging home', the author emphasises the indistinctness of the workers' appearance: the author is suggesting that it is difficult to discern details in how they look, which gives them an air of homogeneity, while also hinting that they are either shrouded in darkness or dark in colour.[1] Moreover, since shadow is a synonym for ghost, it also implies an otherworldliness to the men's appearance.

The examiner is wanting to see close language analysis here: they want the candidate the scratch beyond the surface of the words the author uses and to explore some of the ways the words could be interpreted.

I score my first mark for observing that the word 'shadows' suggests that they are indistinct (after all, shadows almost entirely efface our features, and are hard to tell apart), and a second for noting that it conjures an air of darkness around the men.[2]

My final point, which observes that 'shadows' is a synonym for ghosts and thus gives the men an otherworldly quality, would have also been worth another mark (if I hadn't already maxed out the marks available already!). However, I've gone above and beyond here not only to impress the examiner, but also to demonstrate that there are a number of arguments students could make that would be eligible for marks.

6 (a). 'Suddenly the engine loomed past the house and came to a stop opposite the gate.'

This sentence has been given a paragraph all to itself. Can you suggest why? [1]

> **This sentence has been formatted as a standalone paragraph to place emphasis on the arrival of the train: the train's arrival marks a pivot in the narrative, the entrance of a new character (the grandfather), and the author is attempting to reflect this in the format.**

You will sometimes be asked to explain why an author has chosen a particular moment to start a new paragraph or a new sentence.

More often than not, it is done to emphasize or underscore something that is happening in the story. After all, by starting a new paragraph, the author is creating a visual pause that slows us down, and arguably adds emphasis to what comes immediately after the pause. Paragraphs breaks are often used to reflect a new turn of events, or to mark the transition to a new thought.

Also, authors will sometimes turn a single sentence into a standalone short paragraph. This is also generally done to add emphasis: the idea explored in that short paragraph is visually separated from the rest of the prose, thereby inviting the reader to also pay it greater attention.

6 (b). The story is written in the third person. Why do you think the writer chose to write in this way? (The third person is when a story is told by a narrator, and not by one of the characters in the story). [1]

> **One reason why the author chose to write the story in the third person is perhaps to emphasise the main character's sense of aloofness and isolation. The main character is not named at any point in the story, and, aside from at the very end, is presented as a fairly stern and detached individual (we are told of her 'disillusionment' and the way she speaks 'sternly'). By putting the reader at a remove from her inner monologue, it places us at a distance, reflecting the way this woman arguably seems to hold the world around her at an arm's length emotionally.**

Aside from this, the third person narration also allows the author to preserve more mystery about the character, thereby motivating the reader to continue reading.

The truth is, we do not necessarily know why the author has chosen to use the third person.

The point of this question, though, is not to definitely answer why the author made this choice. It's to put forward a convincing and credible reason that will convince the examiner.

Third person narration, as noted in the question, is when you have a disembodied narrator watching on from above and telling the story. The most common alternative to this is first person narration, which is when one of the characters tells the story ('I did this'; 'I went there').

If we think about it, the first person is a more intimate style: you are right inside the character's head. It is also arguably less flexible: we are unable to jump between the thoughts of different characters. Third person narration is generally more flexible, but it places us at a distance from the characters. We are not inside their head in the same way.

The woman in this text seems to be a somewhat emotionally detached individual, and I argue that this detachment is reflected in the author's choice to opt for a third person narration.

I also very quickly hint at another reason for the third person narration: namely, that it preserves mystery about the woman. This point is not greatly developed in my answer, as I had likely already secured the mark with my first point. That said, if I had developed this argument, it would likely also be eligible for a mark.

The key takeaway here is that there is not a specific argument the examiner is looking for you to make. Rather, the task here is to put forward a credible reason for the author's choice, and to argue it convincingly.

A similar question to this that I have occasionally seen in 10+ papers is to do with tense: a student might be presented with a text in the present tense and be asked why the author made that choice. Generally the present tense is more immediate, and it allows the reader to experience the emotions seemingly at the same time as the characters. In short, you would draw on the nature of the present tense, and how it functions, to argue your point in a similar way to how I have argued my point above.

7. What do you think will happen next? Explain your answer with reference to the passage as a whole. [4]

Given that the final line of the passage sees the train driver address the woman and ask her for a cup of tea ('Have you got a cup of tea?'), we might extrapolate that the woman's next action will be to bring a cup of tea out to the driver. We have also been told that the driver is the woman's son's grandfather, from which we can infer that he is either the woman's father or father-in-law. As such, we might expect the woman and this family patriarch to have a brief heart-to-heart: I would expect the grandfather to ask about his grandson's wellbeing, and for the woman to enquire about his train driving.[3]

I would also expect the woman to bring her son (John) over to greet his grandfather: she has, after all, seemingly beckoned him from the garden ('Come, come on') with the announcement that his grandfather is imminently set to arrive ('There's your grandfather'), which suggests she wants John to come and greet his grandfather. Perhaps the grandfather could jokingly comment on the boy's clothes. The grandfather's 'cheery, hearty' manner of speaking suggests he might be a playful personality; and we know that John's clothes were 'evidently cut down from a man's clothes.' Perhaps these clothes might once have belonged to John's grandfather himself, and perhaps the grandfather might make a jocular comment, gently teasing John's appearance.[4] However, I expect John to take the comments in poor humour: we are told, after all, about his 'resentful, taciturn movement' earlier in the extract, which suggests a sombre mood / personality.

I expect that, after having his tea, the grandfather will continue driving the train. At this point, perhaps we might expect one of the 'workers' we earlier saw walking along the train tracks to appear at the house – perhaps this worker even lives with this woman and John. Earlier, we are told about the woman's appearance of 'disillusionment'. Perhaps this could be the result of some tragedy in her life, and perhaps we might discover that she is a widow. As a result, perhaps the worker that arrives turns out to be John's older brother, who has started working just recently – to help the family make ends meet. We might then have a sequence that sees the mother and two sons sit down for a dinner of eggs from the 'chicken coop' in the garden.

This is one of the trickiest types of questions you're likely to encounter in a 10+ paper – though also arguably the one that also allows you to exercise the greatest degree of creativity, which for many students will feel liberating.

The task at hand is to try and predict what will happen next in the story. Yes, the examiner is looking for candidates to be creative, but, crucially, they will also want your predictions to be based on details from the passage. The trick is to read the passage carefully, take note of granular details about the characters and what they are getting up to, then to extrapolate out from those details. If a character seems comical, then perhaps they will tell a joke later. If a character is walking to a park, then perhaps the next section of the passage is likely to be about what happens at the park. You get the idea.

In my answer, I suggest that the mother takes John over to greet his grandfather. However, another answer might have suggested that, because John seems like a taciturn child, he would have refused to greet his grandfather. Indeed, given that his mother had been suspicious that he had been spending time at the brook, John might even have ended up running away to the brook in order to spite his mother for thinking the worst of him. In other words, so long as the answer given is rooted coherently in the text, the answer will be given credit.

The examiner will not have a specific answer that they are looking to see here. Instead, they will judge your answer: a) on the creativity of your response; and b) on the strength of the justifications you have given for your predictions (with (b) being more important than (a)). And remember, while justifying your predictions, you need to be regularly quoting from the passage.

This question is worth four marks. My response almost certainly goes above and beyond. Nevertheless, you will want to make at least four interesting predictions to be in with a chance of scoring all four marks – and each prediction must have some justification in the text.

<u>Q8 requires a longer, more detailed answer</u>

8. The writer of the story makes frequent mentions of plants and flowers. In what ways does the passage use plants and flowers to create atmosphere? [6]

Refer to details in the text to back up your ideas.

You might write about:

- The plants and flowers described in the first paragraph
- The bush next to which the boy appears
- How the boy treats the chrysanthemums
- How the mother treats the chrysanthemums

The author uses flowers and plants near the start of the passage as a mechanism to enhance the air of disrepair around the 'low cottage'. The

reader is told first of the 'large bony vine' that 'clutched at the house, as if to claw down the tiled roof'. This personified vine is imbued with malicious agency – it is actively seeking to bring down 'the tiled roof' – while the lexicon almost seems to present it as monstrous: it is 'bony' and 'clutche[s]' and 'claw[s]'.[5] The vine, then, both suggests the idea of nature accelerating the house's disrepair, but also lends the house's premises a general air of deprivation through its skeletal portrayal. As other plants are described in the opening chapter, the air of almost skeletal disrepair continues: we hear of the 'twiggly apple trees' – the emphasis on the twigs suggesting just the bare bones of the tree – and of the 'ragged cabbage'. The chrysanthemums, too, are described as 'dishevelled': a word that emphasises a lack of upkeep and again underscores the shabbiness.

If the flora is used to colour our perception of the house, it is also used to help characterise the young boy, John. Crucially, John first appears behind 'raspberry-canes that rose like whips'. That the canes are likened via simile to whips is no coincidence, for it helps emphasise our sense of the strict discipline that seems so central to John's childhood. His mother, while trying to track him down, seeks for John 'piercingly', talks 'sternly', and is accusative in her questioning ('Are you at that brook?'). But if the simile enhances our sense of John's strict upbringing – the way his mother likes to crack the metaphorical whip – the sharpness of these canes could also emphasise the prickliness of his personality: his 'resentful, taciturn' streak.

While the 'raspberry-canes' arguably emphasise an air of tension between mother and son, the way the characters interact with the chrysanthemums arguably hints at an underlying tenderness. We learn that, as they walk towards the house, John 'tore at the ragged wisps of chrysanthemums' – his tearing perhaps an externalisation of his resentment – and, perhaps predictably, this earns him a rebuke from his mother.[6] Yet this rebuke is almost immediately replaced with regret: the mother is 'suddenly pitiful' and breaks off 'three of four wan flowers and held them against her face'. The mother here seems to be obliquely displaying an affection for her son via the chrysanthemums – her pity for her son sublimated into a physical display of affection towards the flowers.[7] That she then tucks it into her 'apron band' emphasises this sense of latent affection: despite her frosty exterior, she wishes to hold her loved one close.

Unsurprisingly, we have an essay-style question to finish off the paper. Notice how the paper is asking us to 'Refer to details in the text to back up your ideas.' As mentioned multiple times, this is a reminder that, when it comes to these essay questions, the examiner wants to see you backing up your arguments with content from the passage, and then dissecting these quotes.

True to form, my first port of call was to put together a quick plan:

- The way in which the plants and flowers colour the perception of the cottage.
- The way the raspberry canes are used to characterise John
- The way the chrysanthemums create an air of tenderness.

Given that six marks were at stake, I decided that three strong, extensively substantiated points would be in order: my intention was for each one of these three points to be scoring me two marks apiece.

You will notice that, as I then put this plan into action, I ended up discussing all of the points that the question told me I 'might' want to write about. Remember, while you don't necessarily need to use these prompts to structure your essay, you should still definitely be paying attention to them all the same.

---

1. If a group of things all look alike, we would call them homogenous. Homogeneity, then, refers to a state of being homogenous.
2. To efface something means to erase or delete it.
3. A patriarch is a father figure – usually one with a certain degree of power and status.
4. A jocular comment is a playful / joking comment.
5. To be malicious is to be evil or malignant in nature.
6. To rebuke someone is to tell them off or chastise them.
7. To do something obliquely is to do it indirectly.
    To sublimate an emotion is to not display it in an obvious way, but instead to let it manifest indirectly through an alternative/unexpected action or behaviour.

Paper Seven: The Multiple Choice Paper (Prose)

All of the papers we have encountered up to this point require us to answer the questions in full sentences – in other words, they are traditional-style comprehension papers. However, there are a handful of schools that administer multiple choice style comprehension papers at 10+. Instead of requesting open-ended answers, the questions in this paper are each followed by four different options: and our task is to select the correct one. In some respects, this style of paper is more straightforward than the ones we have encountered already. However, we must not be complacent, as these papers nevertheless contain some unique difficulties that at times make them just as challenging as the papers we have looked at already!

Mr. Spaceship

THE MULTIPLE CHOICE PAPER (PROSE); 30 MINUTES

This passage is taken from a short story, and set in a fictional version of America.

---

1   For a long time the two of them stood studying the small wood house, overgrown with ivy, set back on the lot behind an enormous oak. The little town was silent and sleepy; once in awhile a truck moved ponderously along the distant highway, but that was all.

5   "This is the place," Gross said to Kramer. He folded his arms. "Quite a quaint little house."

Kramer said nothing. The two Security Agents behind them were expressionless.

Gross started toward the gate. "Let's go. According to the check he's still alive, but very sick. His mind is agile, however. That seems to be certain. It's said he doesn't
10 leave the house. A woman takes care of his needs. He's very frail."

They went down the stone walk and up onto the porch. Gross rang the bell. They waited. After a time they heard slow footsteps. The door opened. An elderly woman in a shapeless wrapper studied them impassively.

"Security," Gross said, showing his card. "We wish to see Professor Thomas."

15 "Why?"

"Government business." He glanced at Kramer.

Kramer stepped forward. "I was a pupil of the Professor's," he said. "I'm sure he won't mind seeing us."

The woman hesitated uncertainly. Gross stepped into the doorway. "This is war time. We can't stand out here."

The two Security agents followed him, and Kramer came reluctantly behind, closing the door. Gross stalked down the hall until he came to an open door. He stopped, looking in. Kramer could see the white corner of a bed, a timber post and the edge of a dresser.

He joined Gross.

In the dark room a withered old man lay, propped up on endless pillows. At first it seemed as if he were asleep; there was no motion or sign of life. But after a time Kramer saw with a faint shock that the old man was watching them intently, his eyes fixed on them, unmoving, unwinking.

"Professor Thomas?" Gross said. "I'm Commander Gross of Security. This man with me is perhaps known to you—"

The faded eyes fixed on Kramer.

"I know him. Philip Kramer…. You've grown heavier, boy." The voice was feeble, the rustle of dry ashes. "Is it true you're married now?"

"Yes. I married Dolores French. You remember her." Kramer came toward the bed. "But we're separated. It didn't work out very well. Our careers—"

"What we came here about, Professor," Gross began, but Kramer cut him off with an impatient wave.

"Let me talk. Can't you and your men get out of here long enough to let me talk to him?"

Gross swallowed. "All right, Kramer." He nodded to the two men. The three of them left the room, going out into the hall and closing the door after them.

The old man in the bed watched Kramer silently. "I don't think much of him," he said at last. "I've seen his type before. What's he want?"

"Nothing. He just came along. Can I sit down?" Kramer found a stiff upright chair beside the bed. "If I'm bothering you—"

"No. I'm glad to see you again, Philip. After so long. I'm sorry your marriage didn't work out."

"How have you been?"

50 "I've been very ill. I'm afraid that my moment on the world's stage has almost ended." The ancient eyes studied the younger man reflectively. "You look as if you have been doing well. Like everyone else I thought highly of. You've gone to the top in this society."

Kramer smiled. Then he became serious. "Professor, there's a project we're working
55 on that I want to talk to you about. It's the first ray of hope we've had in this whole war. If it works, we may be able to crack the Yuk defenses, get some ships into their system. If we can do that the war might be brought to an end."

"Go on. Tell me about it, if you wish."

"It's a long shot, this project. It may not work at all, but we have to give it a try."

60 "It's obvious that you came here because of it," Professor Thomas murmured. "I'm becoming curious. Go on."

An extract adapted from Philip K. Dick's Mr Spaceship

---

1. What kind of phrase is "The little town was silent and sleepy"?

   a) Simile
   b) Symbol
   c) Onomatopoeia
   d) Personification

Answer: ___

2. What kind of movement is suggested by the phrase 'a truck moved ponderously along the distant highway'?

   a) A quick, intelligent movement.
   b) A motion akin to moving through a pond.
   c) A slow, lumbering movement.
   d) A strange, erratic movement.

Answer: ___

3. Which description from the passage makes Professor Thomas' house seem poorly maintained?

   a) Small wood house

b) Overgrown with ivy
   c) Behind an enormous oak
   d) Quaint little house.

Answer: ___

4. What do you think the word "agile" means in this context (line 9)?

   a) Nimble
   b) Full of guile
   c) Mysterious
   d) Fragile

Answer: ___

5. What does the word 'frail' at line 10 mean?

   a) sick
   b) delicate
   c) needy
   d) independent

Answer: ___

6. Look again at lines 8 to 16. What main change takes place in this passage?

   a) The men go from outside the gate to the house to the front door.
   b) The men enter Professor Thomas' house.
   c) The men go from outside Professor Thomas' house to just within the threshold.
   d) The men go from outside the gate of the house to the garden path.

Answer: ___

7. What sort of expression would you expect to see if someone studied you 'impassively'? (line 13)

   a) Angry
   b) Pacifistic
   c) Unemotional
   d) Sneering

8. How does Kramer differ from Gross in how he addresses the woman at the door?

  a) Kramer is a lot less polite than Gross
  b) Unlike Gross, Kramer explains how he knows Professor Thomas
  c) Unlike Gross, Kramer uses his body to emphasise his words.
  d) Unlike Gross, Kramer mentions the war to try and influence the woman.

Answer: ___

9. How are we made aware that Kramer feels some reluctance to enter the house without the woman's permission?

  a) Kramer is silent as he stands outside Thomas' house.
  b) Kramer only enters once Gross does, and exhibits clear hesitancy.
  c) Kramer only speaks to the woman when prompted by Gross.
  d) Kramer spent an unusually long time standing outside Thomas's house.

Answer: ___

10. What impression of Gross is given by the word 'stalked' at line 22?

  a) he is quick
  b) he is extremely powerful
  c) he is very tall
  d) he is predatory

Answer: ___

11. What word could replace 'timber' in the phrase 'the timber post' (line 23)

  a) steel
  b) wooden
  c) tin
  d) long

Answer: ___

12. What technique is the writer using in the following phrase: 'propped up on endless pillows'

a) pun
b) personification
c) simile
d) exaggeration

Answer: ___

13. Why does Kramer get a shock at line 28 when he realises that Professor Thomas was watching him?

a) Because Thomas was not blinking at all, which was unsettling
b) Because Kramer had thought Thomas was asleep
c) Because Kramer had thought Thomas' sight was too poor to see in the dim light.
d) Because the room was so dark that it made seeing anything difficult.

Answer: ___

14. What impression is created of Professor Thomas by the phrase: 'eyes fixed on them, unmoving, unwinking.'

a) He is a jovial, unserious person.
b) He is a watchful yet lazy person.
c) He is a watchful, vigilant person.
d) He is someone with impeccable eyesight.

Answer: ___

15. What technique is the writer using in the following phrase: 'The voice was feeble, the rustle of dry ashes.'

a) Stanza
b) Contrast
c) Flashback
d) Metaphor

Answer: ___

16. Why does Gross leave Professor Thomas' bedroom?

a) Because he wants to interrogate the woman he met at the door.
b) Because Professor Thomas is very frail and Gross is scared of overwhelming him.
c) Because Kramer asked him to, and Kramer is his boss.
d) Because Kramer asked him to, and he feels Kramer will be more effective alone.

Answer: ___

17. What was Professor Thomas' first impression of Gross?

a) Thomas disliked Gross because Gross was rude to the woman at the door.
b) Thomas had a low opinion of Gross – Gross reminded him of others he disliked.
c) Thomas found Gross overly blunt.
d) Thomas disliked that Gross interrupted other people's conversations.

Answer: ___

18. What do you understand of the following phrase at lines 50-51: 'my moment on the world's stage has almost ended'?

a) I am almost approaching the end of my career.
b) I am soon going to be too old to help with world events
c) I can no longer pretend to be something I'm not.
d) I am nearing the end of my life.

Answer: ___

19. What does the word 'ancient' (line 51) mean in this context?

a) prehistoric
b) extremely elderly
c) bloodshot
d) unfocused

Answer: ___

20. What does the line 'reflectively' at line 51 mean?

a) Reflexively
b) Thoughtfully

c) Sadly
d) Morosely

Answer: ___

21. Look again at lines 51 to 53. From what you can infer, does Professor Thomas consider himself a good judge of character?

a) No, because the student he liked has a failed marriage.
b) The passage doesn't say.
c) Yes, as the students he liked best are now the ones he deems most successful.
d) Up to a point. Some of his students have succeeded and he is not surprised.

Answer: ___

22. At line 56, Kramer says the following: 'we may be able to crack the Yuk defenses'. What do you think the word 'Yuk' refers to?

a) A group with whom the government is at war.
b) A group assisting the government in war.
c) Gross and his Security Agents.
d) Professor Thomas.

Answer: ___

23. Look again at line 54 to line 61 at the end of the passage. Which of the following best describes this section of text?

a) Professor Thomas is panicked about ending the war.
b) Kramer is broaching a topic that Professor Thomas seems interested in.
c) Kramer is telling Professor Thomas all the details of his war plans.
d) Kramer is trying to work out whether Professor Thomas can be trusted.

Answer: ___

24. Which of the following best describes the relationship between Kramer and Professor Thomas?

a) Kramer was Professor Thomas' protégé.
b) Kramer studied under Professor Thomas.
c) Kramer and Professor Thomas met through Dolores.

Mr. Spaceship

d) Kramer and Professor Thomas were classmates.

Answer: ___

25. What is the main purpose of this passage?

a) To describe Professor Thomas' house
b) To introduce a new character into an ongoing drama
c) To show how well respected Kramer is in this society.
d) To make Professor Thomas seem like a tragic, hopeless figure.

Answer: ___

Answers & Guidance

1. What kind of phrase is "The little town was silent and sleepy"?

   a) **Simile**
   b) **Symbol**
   c) **Onomatopoeia**
   d) **Personification**

Answer: D

There are two key methods available to us when tackling multiple choice questions: we can either work out the correct answer outright, or we can eliminate the incorrect answers. However, it's often useful to use a **blend** of these two methods. This allows us to double-check our answers when we think we've found the correct one, but also allows us to better our odds by removing incorrect answers when we are unable to figure out the correct answer straight away.

The correct answer here is (d), personification. This is when human attributes are given to non-human or even inanimate things. The town is not a living thing. However, it is being described as 'sleepy' – as though it were a tired human being. As a result, we can plainly see that this is an example of personification.

However, as already mentioned, it can be instructive to also eliminate the other options, so we can feel confident in our choice.

A simile is a linguistic device in which one thing is explicitly compared to another using the word 'like' or 'as'. If the author had written instead that 'the town was as still as a stone', this would have been an example of a simile, as it would be likening the town to a stone using the word 'as'. However, given that neither the words 'like' or 'as' are present here, we can see it is not a simile, and thus (a) is incorrect.

A symbol is, in literature, when something is used to represent something else. For example, let's imagine you have a story where a woman frequently experiences bouts of depression, and the author always seems to mention the full moon when discussing the woman's depression. In that instance, the moon could be considered a symbol of the woman's depression.

Now, it's not impossible that the author is trying to use the town as a symbol. However, there is no particular evidence of this in the phrase we've been asked to look at: **'The little town was silent and sleepy'.** As a result, 'symbol' is a far weaker answer than 'personification', and thus we can safely eliminate option (b).

(A quick side note: I find when dealing with multiple choice questions that it sometimes helps to think of the mission not as one of finding the correct answer, but as one of finding the best answer of the choices available. Remember, while examiners may seem scary, they are human beings, and sometimes their questions are not completely and utterly perfect.)

Onomatopoeia is when you have a word that audibly sounds like the thing it is describing. The word 'sizzle', for instance, sounds similar to when something sizzles. The word 'crash' sounds like the phenomenon of objects colliding. There is no evidence of onomatopoeia in this phrase, so we can also eliminate (c).

2. What kind of movement is suggested by the phrase 'a truck moved ponderously along the distant highway'?

    a) A quick, intelligent movement.
    b) A motion akin to moving through a pond.
    c) A slow, lumbering movement.
    d) A strange, erratic movement.

Answer: C

We are being asked to explain the meaning of a phrase here; but, in reality, the examiner is chiefly trying to establish whether we know what the word 'ponderously' means.

To move ponderously is to move in an awkward, slow, and/or unwieldy fashion. With this in mind, it is plain that that (c) is our correct answer.

However, before pressing on, it is worth our while to pause for a moment to examine how the other options are trying to catch us out.

Option (a) is asserting that 'ponderously' implies a 'quick, intelligent movement'. Some students might be tempted to think that the word 'ponderously' has something to do with the word 'ponder', which means to think / consider things deeply, and might thus assume the truck is moving in a way that somehow indicates intelligence. This is of course incorrect. However, the thing to take away here is that examiners will sometimes try to trip you up by giving you definitions to words that sound similar to the word you are being asked you to define.

Option (b) is trying to catch us out in a similar way. The word 'pond' happens to be the first syllable in the word 'ponderously', and so some students might (wrongly!) assume that 'ponderously' suggests 'a motion akin to moving through a pond'.

Remember to watch out for this kind of trickery in 10+ multiple choice papers: it's more common than you might think!

3. Which description from the passage makes Professor Thomas' house seem poorly maintained?

    a) Small wood house
    b) Overgrown with ivy
    c) Behind an enormous oak
    d) Quaint little house.

Answer: B

We have been given four short phrases here, and we've been asked to identify which one of them portrays Professor Thomas' house as poorly maintained.

Option (a) describes it as a 'small wood house'. The word 'small' does not suggest it is poorly maintained; it only really tells us about its size. The word 'wood' similarly only tells us the material from which it is constructed, and tells us nothing about its condition. We can therefore safely eliminate option (a).

Option (d), like option (a), tells us about the size of the house (it calls it 'little'); and the word 'quaint' suggests it is pretty in an unexpected or unusual way. As a result, we can see that (d) is not the correct answer, either.

Option (c) seems simply to be describing the location of the house – it is 'behind an enormous oak'. It does not, however, tell us anything about the house's level of maintenance; so option (c) can also be eliminated.

Finally, we have option (b), which describes the house as being 'overgrown with ivy'. The word 'overgrown' suggests there is a surplus of ivy on the house: that the ivy has been allowed to envelope the house in a way that goes beyond acceptability. As a result, it clearly seems to suggest that the house is not being well maintained, and thus (b) is our correct answer.

4. What do you think the word "agile" means in this context (line 9)?

   a) **Nimble**
   b) **Full of guile**
   c) **Mysterious**
   d) **Fragile**

Answer: A

Here we have a more straightforward definition-style question. Notice that it is asking us what the word 'agile' means *'in this context'*. This is an acknowledgement that certain words have more than one meaning, and that the context can give us a clue as to which meaning the author is going with.

My advice? Although not all definition-style questions use phrases like 'in this context', I would suggest always keeping in mind how context might impact meaning.

Now, the first step is to re-read how the word is used in the extract:

> 'According to the check he's still alive, but very sick. His mind is agile, however.'

Reading this carefully, we can see that the speaker (Gross) is drawing a contrast between the doctor's physical sickness, and the doctor's 'agile' mind. As a result, we can infer from context that 'fragile' is the incorrect answer, and that 'mysterious' would make little sense; which means we can eliminate options (c) and (d).

The word 'agile' means quick and nimble, so (a) is the correct answer.

Option (b) is another example of the examiner trying to catch us out. To be full of guile means to be full of cunning; so, from context, it could potentially fit. To confuse us further, 'guile' rhymes with 'agile'. However, it in fact means something quite different from 'agile', and thus (b) is another incorrect option.

5. What does the word 'frail' at line 10 mean?

   a) sick
   b) delicate
   c) needy
   d) independent

Answer: B

To be frail means to be very delicate and fragile; hence, option (b) is the correct answer.

If the student does not know the meaning of the word in advance, this question is slightly harder, because we can eliminate fewer options via context alone.

Nevertheless, let's look at the context in which this word appears. Again, it is a word spoken by Gross while discussing Professor Thomas: 'It's said he doesn't leave the house. A woman takes care of his needs. He's very frail.'

At the very least, the context allows us to eliminate option (d); after all, if somebody is taking care of all your needs, it implies that you are the opposite to 'independent'.

Both 'sick' and 'needy' could conceivably work here. This question does not give us as much room to eliminate 'bad' options; instead, the examiner is trying to determine whether the student knows the meaning of the word 'frail' in advance.

6. Look again at lines 8 to 16. What main change takes place in this passage?

   a) The men go from outside the gate to the house to the front door.
   b) The men enter Professor Thomas' house.
   c) The men go from outside Professor Thomas' house to just within the threshold.
   d) The men go from outside the gate of the house to the garden path.

Answer: A

It may sound blindingly obvious, but whenever you're being asked to 'look again' or 'look closely' at a portion of the extract, it's usually a good idea to give the passage another quick skim through.

This question is asking us merely to demonstrate an understanding of what is going on in the plot from lines 8 to 16.

Line 8 starts with the following: 'Gross started toward the gate'. This suggests that the two men at this point in the passage are outside the gate to Thomas' house.

At line 11, we learn that Gross and Kramer go 'up onto the porch', but they go no further than this by the time we get to the end of line 16.

As a result, we can see that option (a) is correct: 'The men go from outside the gate to the house to the front door.'

7. What sort of expression would you expect to see if someone studied you 'impassively'? (line 13)

    a) Angry
    b) Pacifistic
    c) Unemotional
    d) Sneering

Answer: C

To look at someone 'impassively' means to look at them without emotion or without expression. As such, option (c) is the correct answer.

The options most likely to trip students up here is (b), 'pacifistic', since the word sounds fairly similar to 'impassively'. However, to be pacifistic means to be against war, and thus has a totally different meaning!

8. How does Kramer differ from Gross in how he addresses the woman at the door?

    a) Kramer is a lot less polite than Gross

b) Unlike Gross, Kramer explains how he knows Professor Thomas
c) Unlike Gross, Kramer uses his body to emphasise his words.
d) Unlike Gross, Kramer mentions the war to try and influence the woman.

Answer: B

Let's take a look at the passage in question – that is, the short sequence that sees Gross and Kramer addressing the woman at the door:

> "'Security,' Gross said, showing his card. 'We wish to see Professor Thomas.'"

> "'Why?'"

> "'Government business.' He glanced at Kramer."

> Kramer stepped forward. "I was a pupil of the Professor's," he said. "I'm sure he won't mind seeing us.'"

> The woman hesitated uncertainly. Gross stepped into the doorway. "This is war time. We can't stand out here."

Option (a) asserts that 'Kramer is a lot less polite than Gross'. However, if anything, Gross is very curt – he announces himself with the lone word 'security', and meets the woman's follow-up question just as brusquely.[1] Although Kramer, on the other hand, is not exactly polite, phrases such as 'I'm sure he won't mind' suggest that, if anything, he is slightly more polite than Gross. In light of this, (a) is clearly incorrect.

Option (c) asserts that 'unlike Gross, Kramer uses his body to emphasise his words'. However, Gross seems to use his body just as much as Kramer does while speaking – for example, Gross 'show[s] his card' while speaking, and 'stepped into the doorway', which is similar to how Kramer 'stepped forward' just prior to speaking. Accordingly, (c) does not seem to fit.

Option (d) is plainly incorrect. It asserts that 'unlike Gross, Kramer mentions the war to try and influence the woman.' However, it is in fact Gross who mentions to war in order to try and influence the woman: 'This is war time', he says at line 19.

Finally, we have option (b), which asserts that 'unlike Gross, Kramer explains how he knows Professor Thomas'. Sure enough, the first thing Kramer says to the woman is that he 'was a pupil of the Professor's'. As such, we can clearly see that (b) is the correct answer here.

. . .

9. How are we made aware that Kramer feels some reluctance to enter the house without the woman's permission?

   a) Kramer is silent as he stands outside Thomas' house.
   b) Kramer only enters once Gross does, and exhibits clear hesitancy.
   c) Kramer only speaks to the woman when prompted by Gross.
   d) Kramer spent an unusually long time standing outside Thomas's house.

Answer: B

The answer to this question is lurking between lines 19 and 21 of the passage, where we find the following: 'Gross stepped into the doorway…The two Security agents followed him, and Kramer came reluctantly behind.' Kramer seems only willing to enter the house once Gross does so, and the narrator explicitly draws attention to the fact that, even then, Kramer still follows 'reluctantly'.

This tallies closely with option (b), which asserts that we are made aware of Kramer's reluctance by the way 'Kramer only enters [the house] once Gross does, and exhibits clear hesitancy.'

Option (a) is clearly incorrect, as Kramer is not in fact silent while standing outside the house. Option (c) is also wrong, because Kramer in fact addresses the woman without any prompting from Gross.

Option (d) asserts that the author communicates Kramer's reluctance to enter by having him spend an 'unusually long time standing outside Thomas's house'. Whether or not he stands outside Thomas's house for an 'unusually' long time is subjective, but there is no indication in the text that he lingers for a very long time. As such, this is plainly a far weaker answer than (b) – and, therefore, (d) can also be eliminated.

10. What impression of Gross is given by the word 'stalked' at line 22?

   a) he is quick
   b) he is extremely powerful
   c) he is very tall

Answers & Guidance

   d) he is predatory

Answer: D

The word 'stalked' appears at line 22, where we read the following: 'Gross stalked down the hall until he came to an open door. He stopped, looking in.'

To stalk someone or something is to follow them in a stealthy manner – it is often used to describe the way in which a predator follows and tracks its prey as it prepares to pounce. With this in mind, option (d) stands out as the answer that fits best.

Option (c) is trying to catch us out. The stalk of a plant is long and tall. Some students might get confused and think that the verb 'stalked' has something to do with a plant stalk, and thus that it is suggesting that Gross is 'very tall'. This is incorrect. Watch out for these sneaky red-herrings!

11. What word could replace 'timber' in the phrase 'the timber post' (line 23)

   a) steel
   b) wooden
   c) tin
   d) long

Answer: B

The word 'timber' appears in a sentence at line 23, which reads as follows: 'Kramer could see the white corner of a bed, a timber post and the edge of a dresser.'

Timber is the processed wood taken from trees. The examiner is, in short, testing to see whether the candidate has this word in their vocabulary; hence, (b) is the correct answer.

12. What technique is the writer using in the following phrase: 'propped up on endless pillows'

   a) pun

b) **personification**
   c) **simile**
   d) **exaggeration**

Answer: D

Let's look at the sentence in which this phrase appears: 'In the dark room a withered old man lay, propped up on endless pillows.'

As I've mentioned already, personification is when human attributes are given to non-human or even inanimate things. However, the pillows here are not being given human attributes; so we can safely eliminate option (b).

We have also already encountered the concept of the simile before, which is when one thing is explicitly compared to another using the word 'like' or 'as'. Again, neither 'like' nor 'as' appears in this phrase, and there is no comparison being invoked, so we can see that this is not a simile, and thus (c) can also be eliminated.

A pun is a type of play on words. To illustrate, there is an old joke that goes as follows:

'Excuse me sir, are you a piece of string?'

'No, I'm a frayed knot.'

The phrase 'frayed knot' sounds almost indistinguishable to the expression 'afraid not' – a common phrase people say after the word 'no'. This is an example, then, of a pun.

There is no such joke in the phrase mentioned in the question; as a result, (a) is incorrect.

Finally, we have option (d), exaggeration. Exaggeration is when you describe something in an over-the-top way that adds emphasis. There are of course not really 'endless' pillows on Professor Thomas' bed – there will of course be a finite number; however, the author is using exaggeration to emphasise the fact that there were many, many pillows. Accordingly, option (d), exaggeration, is correct.

13. Why does Kramer get a shock at line 28 when he realises that Professor Thomas was watching him?

   a) **Because Thomas was not blinking at all, which was unsettling**

b) **Because Kramer had thought Thomas was asleep**
c) **Because Kramer had thought Thomas' sight was too poor to see in the dim light.**
d) **Because the room was so dark that it made seeing anything difficult.**

Answer: B

Between lines 26 and 28 we encounter the following text: 'At first it seemed as if he were asleep; there was no motion or sign of life. But after a time Kramer saw with a faint shock that the old man was watching them intently…'.

We can see that, at first, Kramer thinks that Professor Thomas is asleep ('it seemed as if he were asleep'). In the very next sentence, we then read how Kramer gets a 'shock' when he sees that Professor Thomas is in fact 'watching them intently'. The flow of these sentences imply that Kramer's shock is induced by the fact that he had not been expecting Thomas to be watching him, since he had assumed Thomas to be sleeping. This closely tallies with option (b) – which is the correct answer.

Option (a) is the one most likely to trip students up. It asserts that Kramer is shocked when he realises Professor Thomas was watching him because 'Thomas was not blinking at all'. It is true that Thomas does not appear to be blinking ('his eyes [were] fixed on them, unmoving, unwinking'). However, it is pretty plain that this was *not* the thing that actually shocked Kramer. As such, option (a) is in fact incorrect.

14. What impression is created of Professor Thomas by the phrase: 'eyes fixed on them, unmoving, unwinking.'

a) **He is a jovial, unserious person.**
b) **He is a watchful yet lazy person.**
c) **He is a watchful, vigilant person.**
d) **He is someone with impeccable eyesight.**

Answer: C

Here we are being asked to look at a specific description of Professor Thomas – namely, the way 'his eyes fixed on them, unmoving, unwinking' – and to infer what this most likely suggests about Thomas himself.

Option (a) argues that it creates an impression of Professor Thomas as being 'jovial' – in other words, cheerful – and 'unserious'. This strongly clashes with the air of seriousness created by Thomas' intense stare.

Option (d) suggests that this description portrays Thomas as 'someone with impeccable eyesight'. However, the description really tells us little about the quality of Thomas' eyesight. Indeed, if anything, the fact he feels the need to watch in such an 'unmoving, unwinking' way – the fact he needs to hold his gaze steady – might suggest that his eyesight is poor. As such, option (d) can be eliminated.

Option (b) describes Thomas as 'watchful', which means something akin to observant and vigilant, and this certainly seems to fit. However, it also describes Thomas as lazy. Although he is 'unmoving', the idea that he is 'unwinking' does not particularly suggest laziness. If anything, it takes effort to vigilantly observe. Moreover, we know from the broader context that Thomas is not in bed because he is lazy, but because he is sick. As a result, 'lazy' does not seem to fit.

Option (c), however, also identifies Thomas as 'watchful', but it accompanies this adjective with the word 'vigilant', which we know is a word with similar connotations to 'watchful': to be vigilant is to maintain awareness of one's surroundings and to be on guard. This certainly seems to capture the impression we get of Thomas with his unwavering gaze, and thus option (c) stands out as our best fit here.

15. What technique is the writer using in the following phrase: 'The voice was feeble, the rustle of dry ashes.'

    a) Stanza
    b) Contrast
    c) Flashback
    d) Metaphor

Answer: D

The correct answer here is (d) – the phrase in question is an example of a metaphor.

What is a metaphor? Many of you will know the answer to this already, but let's quickly recap.

A metaphor is a linguistic device in which one thing is implicitly compared or likened to another thing. It is similar to another technical device we have already encountered, the simile, which is when one thing is explicitly compared to another using the word 'like' or 'as'.

Let's briefly look at the difference between the two.

If I were to say: 'The pain felt like fire coursing through my body', this would be a simile, because I am using the word 'like' to compare my pain to fire.

However, if I were instead to say: 'The pain was a fire coursing through my body', this would be a metaphor. I'm still likening my pain to fire, but this time I'm not using the word 'like' and 'as' to make that comparison explicit.

Technically speaking, a simile is a type of metaphor; but for the sake of 10+ exams, it's best to think of them as two separate entities.

Let's now take a look at the phrase this question is actually asking us about: 'The voice was feeble, the rustle of dry ashes'. Here, Thomas' voice is being likened to 'the rustle of dry ashes', but the author is not using the word 'like' or 'as' to make that comparison explicit. As a result, we know that it is a metaphor, and that option (d) is therefore correct.

Let's quickly run through the other terms we have been presented with here.

A stanza is what we call a paragraph in a poem. This term clearly has nothing to do with the phrase we are being asked about; therefore, (a) can be eliminated.

Contrast is when two things are dramatically different from one another. Thomas' voice does not stand in contrast to dry ashes: instead, they are alike. Accordingly, we can see that option (b) is incorrect.

A flashback – option (c) – is when a narrative pauses to explore events from an earlier period of time, and clearly this term has no relevance to the phrase in question.

16. Why does Gross leave Professor Thomas' bedroom?

    a) **Because he wants to interrogate the woman he met at the door.**
    b) **Because Professor Thomas is very frail and Gross is scared of overwhelming him.**
    c) **Because Kramer asked him to, and Kramer is his boss.**
    d) **Because Kramer asked him to, and he feels Kramer will be more effective alone.**

Answer: D

This is in some respects the trickiest question in this paper so far, because it is asking us to exercise our inference skills. However, we can make life easier for ourselves by using the process of elimination.

The pivotal passage can be found between lines 37 and 42. I shall reproduce it here:

> "What we came here about, Professor," Gross began, but Kramer cut him off with an impatient wave.
>
> "Let me talk. Can't you and your men get out of here long enough to let me talk to him?"
>
> Gross swallowed. "All right, Kramer." He nodded to the two men. The three of them left the room, going out into the hall and closing the door after them.

Option (a) suggests that Gross leaves Thomas' bedroom 'because he wants to interrogate the woman he met at the door'. There is zero evidence that this is why Gross leaves the room, and thus option (a) can easily be dismissed.

Option (c) suggests that Gross leaves because Kramer asks him to, and Kramer is his boss. It is true that Kramer asks Gross to leave ('Can't you and your men get out of here long enough to let me talk to him?'), but there is no evidence whatsoever that Kramer is Gross's boss. Rather, it seems that Gross is high up with the country's security apparatus, and Kramer is one of Thomas' previous students. It seems, then, that neither one is the other's boss, and thus option (c) does not seem to fit.

This leaves us with options (b) and (d).

Option (b) argues that Gross leaves because 'Thomas is very frail and Gross is scared of overwhelming him'. It is difficult to know definitively whether Gross is scared of overwhelming Thomas; however, given that Gross has barged into Thomas' house and has brought two further henchmen with him, one might be sceptical that this is the case.

On the other hand, we have option (d), which contests that Gross leaves because 'Kramer asked him to, and he feels Kramer will be more effective alone.'

As mentioned already, Kramer does in fact ask Gross to leave. But, crucially, it would certainly seem that Gross' priority is indeed extracting information from Thomas – after all, it appears he is there as part of a war effort ('This is war time', he says to the woman at the door); and Kramer's line of conversation later in the passage seems to confirm that they are there to pick Thomas' brain about the war.

With all this in mind, it seems far more convincing that Gross leaves because he feels that leaving Kramer to talk to Thomas alone will allow them to extract information more efficiently – and *not* because he is especially concerned about overwhelming Kramer. And, sure enough, option (d) is the answer the examiner is looking for.

17. What was Professor Thomas' first impression of Gross?

    a) Thomas disliked Gross because Gross was rude to the woman at the door.
    b) Thomas had a low opinion of Gross – Gross reminded him of others he disliked.
    c) Thomas found Gross overly blunt.
    d) Thomas disliked that Gross interrupted other people's conversations.

Answer: B

The key to this question can be found at lines 43 to 44, where we have Thomas explicitly giving his thoughts on Gross to Kramer:

"'I don't think much of him,' he said at last. 'I've seen his type before.'"

The first comment – 'I don't think much of him' – does not narrow things down much, since all four of our options suggest that Thomas disliked Gross. Thomas' second comment, though – that he has 'seen [Gross'] type before' – points us towards option (b) : Thomas is saying that Gross reminds him of other people he'd met in the past whom he had disliked.

The other three options try to trip us up by focusing on other unlikeable characteristics about Gross that we do indeed see in the text; however, these are not things that Thomas mentions when telling Kramer his first impressions of Gross.

18. What do you understand of the following phrase at lines 50-51: 'my moment on the world's stage has almost ended'?

    a) I am almost approaching the end of my career.
    b) I am soon going to be too old to help with world events
    c) I can no longer pretend to be something I'm not.
    d) I am nearing the end of my life.

When Thomas at lines 50-51 asserts that his 'moment on the world's stage has almost ended', he is using a metaphor.

In short, he is likening life to a performance on a stage. By saying that his 'moment' on this stage is 'almost ended', he is saying that he has very little time left to live. As a result, option (d) is correct.

19. What does the word 'ancient' (line 51) mean in this context?

    a) prehistoric
    b) extremely elderly
    c) bloodshot
    d) unfocused

Answer: B

This is a definition question that demonstrates the importance of context.

The word 'ancient' appears in a sentence that describes Thomas' eyes as he observes Kramer: 'The ancient eyes studied the younger man reflectively.'

One valid definition of 'ancient' is that it describes something from the distant past, a past that no longer exists; and option (a) – 'prehistoric' – seems to best match this particular definition of the word.

However, 'ancient' can also be used as a hyperbolic term, used to describe something or someone that is old or elderly in exaggerated terms. Thomas clearly still exists; rather, the author is using the term 'ancient' to hyperbolically emphasise that Thomas is extremely elderly. As a result, option (b) is in fact the correct answer here.

20. What does the line 'reflectively' at line 51 mean?

    a) Reflexively
    b) Thoughtfully
    c) Sadly
    d) Morosely

Answers & Guidance

Answer: B

To do something 'reflectively' is to do it in a thoughtful or contemplative way; therefore, option (b) is the correct answer.

Option (a) is trying to catch us out: it is giving us a word – 'reflexively' – that sounds fairly similar to the word we are being asked to define. However, it has a totally different meaning: to do something reflexively is to do something as if by reflex / without premeditated thought.

21. Look again at lines 51 to 53. From what you can infer, does Professor Thomas consider himself a good judge of character?

   a) No, because the student he liked has a failed marriage.
   b) The passage doesn't say.
   c) Yes, as the students he liked best are now the ones he deems most successful.
   d) Up to a point. Some of his students have succeeded and he is not surprised.

Answer: C

The question here is asking us to 'infer', which means to look for something that is implicit as opposed to explicit. Let's take a close look at the relevant passage:

> "You look as if you have been doing well. Like everyone else I thought highly of. You've gone to the top in this society."

Thomas, here, first asserts that, as far as he can see, Kramer – his former student – 'is doing well'. Then, in the very next sentence, he suggests that this is something Kramer has in common with 'everyone else [Thomas] thought highly of'.

Although Thomas is not explicitly calling himself a good judge of character, the very fact he is pointing out that all the students he liked have 'been doing well' – and have gone 'to the top of society' – implicitly suggests that Thomas sees himself as having capably identified the most talented people in advance. From this we can infer that he sees himself as a good judge of character, thereby pointing us towards option (c) – which is the correct answer.

22. At line 56, Kramer says the following: 'we may be able to crack the Yuk defenses'. What do you think the word 'Yuk' refers to?

a) A group with whom the government is at war.
b) A group assisting the government in war.
c) Gross and his Security Agents.
d) Professor Thomas.

Answer: A

The answer the examiner is looking for here is (a), which asserts that the word 'Yuk' would appear to refer to 'a group with whom the government is at war'.

Let's first take a look at Kramer's comment in context. It appears during his private conversation with Thomas near the end of the extract:

> "Professor, there's a project we're working on that I want to talk to you about. It's the first ray of hope we've had in this whole war. If it works, we may be able to crack the Yuk defenses, get some ships into their system. If we can do that the war might be brought to an end."

It has already been indicated that Kramer and Gross are paying a visit to Thomas against the backdrop of an ongoing war: after all, when Gross addresses the woman at the door, he says 'This is war time'. Moreover, in the passage quoted above, Kramer claims that if they are 'able to crack the Yuk defenses' then 'the war might be brought to an end.'

With all this in mind, we can start to eliminate some options. It would seem that 'Yuk' does not refer to Professor Thomas; after all, Professor Thomas is the individual Kramer is talking to, and Kramer is clearly talking about a third party. Option (d), then, can be eliminated.

Furthermore, it is plain that Gross is working alongside Kramer in this war effort: indeed, the entire plot trajectory of the passage seems to be the pair of them working together in order to pick Thomas' brain as part of this war effort. As a result, we can see that 'Yuk' does not refer to 'Gross and his Security Agents', so option (c) can also be dismissed.

Option (b) suggests that 'Yuk' might refer to 'a group assisting the government in war'.

We know that Gross works for the government ('Government business,' he tells the woman at the door), and that Kramer and Gross are on the same side. However, Kramer portrays the entity known as 'Yuk' as the government's antagonists: he wants to 'crack' their 'defenses' and get 'ships into their system' in order to end the war.

This would suggest that 'Yuk' is *not* an entity assisting the government in war; rather, it is an entity at war with the government. This allows us to dismiss option (b), and points us in the direction of option (a) – the correct answer.

23. Look again at line 54 to line 61 at the end of the passage. Which of the following best describes this section of text?

   a) Professor Thomas is panicked about ending the war.
   b) Kramer is broaching a topic that Professor Thomas seems
      interested in.
   c) Kramer is telling Professor Thomas all the details of his war
      plans.
   d) Kramer is trying to work out whether Professor Thomas can be
      trusted.

Answer: B

During this section of text, Kramer starts to discuss a project that might allow them to win the war against the Yuk – though he does not yet delve into specifics – and, judging by the very final line, it would appear that the discussion has piqued Thomas' interest: 'I'm becoming curious. Go on.'

This firmly points us in the direction of option (b), since Kramer is indeed 'broaching a topic that Professor Thomas seems interested in.'

To remove any doubt, let's quickly run through the other options.

There is no evidence that Thomas is panicked about the end of the war, so (a) is patently incorrect.

Kramer does not tell Thomas all the details of his war plans. He merely states that they have a plan, and Thomas, at the very end of the extract, invites him to 'go on.' As such, option (c) can also be eliminated.

Finally, there seems to be no ambiguity whether or not Kramer thinks Thomas can be trusted. Rather, it seems as though he trusts Thomas implicitly. In light of this, we can safely eliminate option (d) as well.

24. Which of the following best describes the relationship between Kramer and Professor Thomas?

a) Kramer was Professor Thomas' protégé.
b) Kramer studied under Professor Thomas.
c) Kramer and Professor Thomas met through Dolores.
d) Kramer and Professor Thomas were classmates.

Answer: B

This question involves straightforward retrieval skills.

At line 17, Kramer says the following to the woman at the door: 'I was a pupil of the Professor's'. This tallies with option (b), which suggests that 'Kramer studied under Professor Thomas'.

25. What is the main purpose of this passage?

a) To describe Professor Thomas' house
b) To introduce a new character into an ongoing drama
c) To show how well respected Kramer is in this society.
d) To make Professor Thomas seem like a tragic, hopeless figure.

Answer: B

This question is quite different to what we have seen already, because it is not asking us directly about the content, but about what we believe the author's intentions to be.

Now, people will often fiercely debate an author's intentions when studying literature. As a result, having a multiple choice question on it, where we have to identify a definitive 'correct' answer, is (in my opinion) quite strange – after all, how can we say for sure what the author's intentions are? However, questions like this *do* occasionally appear in 10+ papers, and we are here to score marks, and not to debate the examiner.

This is one of those occasions, then, where it is best to think of our task as looking for the best answer of the bunch. So let's dive in.

Option (a) suggests that the main purpose of the passage is to 'describe Professor Thomas' house'. It certainly true that there are moments when the narrative does take time to describe Thomas' house. However, this accounts for a very small proportion of the total text, and, as a result, this does not feel like a strong option.

Option (b) suggests that the main purpose of the passage is to 'introduce a new character into an ongoing drama.' At the very start of the extract, there seems to be two significant characters – Kramer and Gross – and the very first sentence puts them front and centre: 'For a long time the two of them stood studying the small wood house.' Shortly after, Gross makes it clear that they are at the house in order to meet somebody in particular, and this individual is the sole subject of their conversation: 'According to the check he's still alive, but very sick,' Gross says to Kramer outside the house. The rest of the passage revolves around the pair then meeting this character – Professor Thomas.

There also appears to be ongoing drama in the form of a war – 'This is war time', Gross says to the woman at the door' – and it seems apparent from Kramer's comments to Thomas near the end of the passage that he wants to pick Thomas' brains regarding a plan they have for the war, thereby inserting Thomas into the ongoing drama.

With all this in mind, option (b) seems like a very strong answer. The passage spends plenty of time introducing a new character – Professor Thomas – and, near the end, seems to insert him in the drama.

Option (c) suggests that the purpose of the passage 'to show how well respected Kramer is in this society.' It is true that Gross seems to respect Kramer enough to obey his request to depart the room at lines 39 to 40, and Professor Thomas at lines 52 to 53 says that Kramer has gone to the 'top of society.' Yet while there is evidence in the text to substantiate the idea that Kramer is well respected in society, it is alluded to briefly just twice, and thus it seems a stretch to suggest that this is the purpose of the entire passage.

Option (d) suggests that the purpose of the extract is 'to make Professor Thomas seem like a tragic, hopeless figure'. One could definitely argue that there is an air of tragedy about him: he is, after all, a professor with an 'agile' mind, who has been laid so low as to be bedridden, and he suggests that he has not long to live at lines 51 to 52. Moreover, Thomas' decrepit state is something that is alluded to throughout the passage.

Yet the very fact that Kramer and Gross are seeking him out suggests that he is not intended to be seen as a completely hopeless figure; rather, the insinuation is that his counsel might be a source of hope during a time of war, and that seems to weaken option (d). Furthermore, Thomas appears to be an old man, and there is no particular indication that he has been laid low as a result of tragic circumstances. Can decrepitude in old age truly be considered tragic? Or is it merely the natural course of things? This line of thinking also weakens option (d).

In short, while option (d) seems like a stronger option than (c) and (a), option (b) continues to stand out as by far the best fit for the passage.

---

1. To be curt is to be rudely abrupt and blunt in conversation. Brusque has a similar meaning!

Paper Eight: The Multiple Choice Paper (Poetry)

This paper very closely resembles the previous one. The key difference is that we are not being asked us to engage with a piece of prose, but with a piece of poetry instead.

I would say that poetry comprehension papers are a good deal rarer than prose papers. That said, some schools do favour them. And do keep in mind that schools are liable to change their style of paper from year to year – I have seen certain schools who have historically favoured prose comprehensions shift to poetry without warning – and we want to be prepared for all eventualities.

Generally speaking, poetry papers tend to have fewer questions in total than prose papers, if only because poems are usually shorter than prose pieces. This is nothing to stress about; it's just another quirk to be aware of.

Finally, a quick note about poetry itself. Many students find the thought of engaging with a poem intimidating. My advice is to keep a cool head, read through the text multiple times, and to accept that there might be words or phrases that the poet has intentionally made difficult – or even impossible – to fully understand. My other advice is to always be asking yourself: does the poet mean this literally or metaphorically?

Summer-like for an Instant

1   Summer-like for an instant the autumn sun bursts out,
    And the light through the turning elms is green and clear,
    It slants down the path and the ragged marigolds glow
    Fiery again, last flames of the dying year.

5   A blue-tit darts with a flash of wings, to feed
    Where the coconut hangs on the pear tree over the wall;
    He digs at the meat like a tiny pickaxe tapping
    With his needle-sharp beak as he clings to the swinging ball.

    Then he runs up the trunk, sure footed and sleek like a mouse,
10 And perches to sun himself; all his body and brain
    Exalt in the sudden sunlight, gladly believing
    That the cold is over and summer is here again.

    But I see the umber clouds that drive for the sun
    And a sorrow no argument ever can take away
15 Goes through my heart as I think of the nearing winter,
    And the transient light that gleams like the ghost of May.

    And the bird, unaware, blessing the summer eternal,
    Joyfully labouring, proud of his strength, gay-plumed,
    Unaware of the hawk and the snow and the frost-bound nights,
20 And his death foredoomed.

George Orwell

1. This poem is set during which time of year?

a) Summer
b) Autumn
c) May
d) December

Answer: ___

2. 'Ragged' (line 3) means:

a) Yellow
b) Full of rage
c) Colourful
d) Unkempt

Answer: ___

3. In line 4, when the poem talks about the 'last flames of the dying year', he is suggesting that:

a) this is the last forest fire of the year.
b) this is the absolute last of any kind of sunlight for the rest of the year.
c) this is the last time the marigolds will be in such intense sunshine this year.
d) the sunlight has created a forest fire for the final time this year.

Answer: ___

4. At lines 5 to 8, the blue-tit is seen feeding on:

a) a pear
b) meat placed within a coconut shell
c) coconut milk
d) a swinging ball that the poet is unable to identify

Answer: ___

5. 'Perches to sun himself' suggests:

a) that the blue-tit has metaphorically purchased time in the sun
b) that the blue-tit is resting and basking in the sun.
c) that a personified sun is sitting next to the blue-tit.
d) that the blue-tit is sitting with a mouse in the sun.

Answer: ___

6. At lines 17 to 18, the blue-tit is 'blessing the summer eternal, / Joyfully labouring'. This suggests:

a) The blue-tit is enjoying the sun and preparing to lay eggs.
b) The blue-tit considers it a blessing to lay eggs in the sun.
c) The blue-tit enjoys her work while basking in an unseasonable sunlight.
d) The summer will never end and the blue-tit is blessing this turn of events.

Answer: ___

7. A 'sorrow no argument ever can take away' goes through the poet's heart because:

a) dark clouds are about to block the sun, ruining the blue-tit's day.
b) he is aware that the blue-tit will soon be hunted by an eagle.
c) he is aware of the impending arrival of winter.
d) this is the last time he will see this blue-tit.

Answer: ___

8. The last two lines of the poem tell us that:

a) the blue-tit is unaware that he will soon face mortal danger
b) the poet has seen a hawk that will hunt the blue-tit in winter.
c) the hawk is unaware that it will soon be winter, and that he will then be doomed.
d) the blue-tit is unaware that there is a prophecy that says he will be doomed.

Answer: ___

9. The form of this poem is best described as:

a) five four-line stanzas with no rhyme scheme
b) a collection of rhyming limericks
c) five four-line stanzas written in rhyming couplets

d) five four-line stanzas with the second and fourth line rhyming.

Answer: ___

10. Overall the feeling of the poem is best described as:

a) a happy memory from childhood
b) a reflection on the bitter-sweet final moments of autumn
c) a comical reflection on the ignorance of a blue-tit who thinks that he is invincible.
d) a strong argument in favour of daylight saving time.

Answer: ___

Answers & Guidance

1. This poem is set during which time of year?

   a) **Summer**
   b) **Autumn**
   c) **May**
   d) **December**

Answer: B

There are many signs that the correct answer is option (b), 'autumn', though the poem's opening line arguably gives us everything we need:

> Summer-like for an instant the autumn sun bursts out

The sun is described as 'the autumn sun', the word 'autumn' being used as an adjective to communicate that this is the sun that one encounters during autumn.

The phrase 'summer-like' will undoubtedly confuse some students. The speaker is not, however, saying that this is summer. Instead, he is saying that this is autumn, but the sun has 'burst out' in such a way that 'for an instant' makes it feel like summer – the intensity of the sun has made things feel 'Summer-like'. Indeed, this whole poem is about a moment in autumn that briefly feels like a slice of summer!

. . .

2. 'Ragged' (line 3) means:

   a) **Yellow**
   b) **Full of rage**
   c) **Colourful**
   d) **Unkempt**

Answer: D

The word 'ragged' means shabby, untidy or unkempt, and thus option (d) very plainly stands out as the correct answer.

Nevertheless, let's take a look at line 3, where the word appears, and take a moment to eliminate the other options:

   It slants down the path and the ragged marigolds glow

Marigolds happen to be orange and yellow, and option (a) is looking to catch out students who perhaps do not know what the word 'ragged' means, but happen to be familiar with the colour of marigolds. After all, if you replace the word 'ragged' with 'yellow', the line would still make sense. As ever, watch out for these plausible yet incorrect options that are designed to trip us up.

The word colourful – option (c) – could similarly be slotted in instead of 'ragged' and the line would still make sense. Again, though, this is not the correct definition of 'ragged'.

Option (b) is trying to trip us up in a different way. The word 'ragged' contains all the same letters as 'rage' (plus an extra 'g' and an extra 'd') and some students might therefore assume they have a similar meaning; however, this is most certainly not the case, and so (b), too, can be eliminated.

Unsurprisingly, the only answer left standing is (d), unkempt, which is precisely the one the examiner is looking for!

3. In line 4, when the poem talks about the 'last flames of the dying year', he is suggesting that:

   a) **this is the last forest fire of the year.**

    b) this is the absolute last of any kind of sunlight for the rest of the year.
    c) this is the last time the marigolds will be in such intense sunshine this year.
    d) the sunlight has created a forest fire for the final time this year.

Answer: C

The correct answer here is (c): the speaker is suggesting in line 4 that this is the last time the marigolds will be exposed to such intense sunshine this year.

Let's take a look at the poem's opening stanza, as this will help us understand how we came to this answer:

> Summer-like for an instant the autumn sun bursts out,
> And the light through the turning elms is green and clear,
> It slants down the path and the ragged marigolds glow
> Fiery again, last flames of the dying year.

Reading carefully, we can see that the 'light' mentioned in line 2 is light from the 'sun' that 'bursts out' in line 1. In line 3, we are then told how this light 'slants down the path and the ragged marigolds glow', the implication being that the light has struck the marigolds, which has then made them to seem to 'glow'. Indeed, given that marigolds are yellow and orange, one might be able to picture how these flowers might seem to 'glow' when in direct sunlight.

In line 4, then, the speaker is still describing these marigolds, and, using a metaphor, he likens their visual appearance in the sun to fire: 'fiery again, last flames of the dying year'. This is not a literal fire. Rather, the marigolds look almost as though they are flames when exposed to the sun.

That we know this is not a literal fire allows us to eliminate options (a) and (d), both of which talk about forest fires.

Option (b) is a bit trickier to dismiss; however, if we look closely, we see that it is saying something more extreme than the poem. The poem is not necessarily saying this is the 'last of any kind of sunlight for the rest of the year.' Rather, it is saying that this is the last of a certain type of intense 'summer-like' sunlight for the year.

Sure enough, option (c) – the only remaining option, and the correct answer – captures this nuance. By asserting that the phrase 'last flames of the dying year' suggests that this is the 'last time the marigolds will be in such intense sunshine this year', it correctly captures the gist of the line. This is the last time the sunlight will be intense enough to make the marigolds glow so brightly as to look like fire.

4. At lines 5 to 8, the blue-tit is seen feeding on:

   a) a pear
   b) meat placed within a coconut shell
   c) coconut milk
   d) a swinging ball that the poet is unable to identify

Answer: B

The correct answer here is (b): the blue-tit is feeding on meat that has been placed within a coconut shell.

This question at first glance appears to be a straightforward retrieval question, yet is in fact a bit trickier than we might expect.

Let's take a look at the second stanza in its entirety:

> A blue-tit darts with a flash of wings, to feed
> Where the coconut hangs on the pear tree over the wall;
> He digs at the meat like a tiny pickaxe tapping
> With his needle-sharp beak as he clings to the swinging ball.

We learn that the blue tit goes 'to feed / Where the coconut hangs on the pear tree'. This suggests that the blue-tit is interacting with the coconut hanging in the pear tree, not with any fruit that the pear tree has produced. That the blue-tit is described as 'cling[ing] to the swinging ball' confirms this deduction, as the 'swinging ball' is clearly a reference to the coconut. As a result, we can eliminate option (a): the blue-tit does not seem to be feeding on a pear.

Option (d) suggests that the poet 'is unable to identify' the swinging ball mentioned at the end of this stanza. However, as we have just said, this ball is very clearly the coconut mentioned in the stanza's second line, meaning we can eliminate (d), too.

In the third line of the stanza, we are told that that the blue-tit 'digs at the meat' while on the coconut. This tells us that the blue-tit is feeding on meat, not coconut milk, and thus the answer is (b) and not (c).

Answers & Guidance

This question perhaps unfairly helps candidates who are already aware that people in the British countryside sometimes put meat in coconuts for blue-tits to feed on. Students who are not aware of this might have thought that the word 'meat' was being used metaphorically to describe the substance inside of a coconut. A clue that this is not correct, however, is that 'meat' is generally solid, whereas coconut milk is a liquid.

5. 'Perches to sun himself' suggests:

    a) that the blue-tit has metaphorically purchased time in the sun
    b) that the blue-tit is resting and basking in the sun.
    c) that a personified sun is sitting next to the blue-tit.
    d) that the blue-tit is sitting with a mouse in the sun.

Answer: B

To perch is to rest or sit. To sun oneself is to bask or relax in the sun. With this in mind, option (b) is very plainly the correct answer.

6. At lines 17 to 18, the blue-tit is 'blessing the summer eternal, / Joyfully labouring'. This suggests:

    a) The blue-tit is enjoying the sun and preparing to lay eggs.
    b) The blue-tit considers it a blessing to lay eggs in the sun.
    c) The blue-tit enjoys her work while basking in an unseasonable sunlight.
    d) The summer will never end and the blue-tit is blessing this turn of events.

Answer: C

The line in question says that the blue-tit is 'blessing the summer eternal'. This suggests that the blue-tit is not only enjoying the sun, but seems to believe that this summer weather will last forever.

However, just because the blue-tit believes the summer will last forever, this does not mean that the line is necessarily saying that this is actually true (in fact, the poem as a whole is about how this is the last of the summer-like weather). So we can eliminate option (d): this line is *not* suggesting that 'the summer will never end', even if it is suggesting that the blue-tit might think this is the case.

The phrase 'joyfully labouring' suggests that the blue-tit is working in a joyful way.

Options (a) and (b), however, are trying to trip us up. Although the poet has used the word labour as a synonym for work, the phrase 'to go into labour' is an expression that means to give birth; and, because of this, some candidates might get confused and think that the speaker is trying to say that the blue-tit is laying eggs. However, this is not the case: in fact, at no moment in the poem does the speaker suggest that the blue-tit is laying eggs.

Accordingly, we can eliminate both (a) and (b).

This leaves us with (c), 'the blue-tit enjoys her work while basking in an unseasonable sunlight.' We have already mentioned that 'joyfully labouring' suggests that the blue-tit enjoys her work. That she is 'blessing the summer eternal' may suggest that the blue-tit thinks the summer will last forever, but it also implies that the blue-tit is enjoying working / basking in this sunlight, which we understand from the wider poem to be an unseasonable spell of weather.

Therefore, option (c) is a very fitting inference, and is the correct answer here.

7. A 'sorrow no argument ever can take away' goes through the poet's heart because:

    a) dark clouds are about to block the sun, ruining the blue-tit's day.
    b) he is aware that the blue-tit will soon be hunted by an eagle.
    c) he is aware of the impending arrival of winter.
    d) this is the last time he will see this blue-tit.

Answer: C

Let's quote the poem's penultimate stanza in its entirety, as this will help us decode this question:

    But I see the umber clouds that drive for the sun

And a sorrow no argument ever can take away
Goes through my heart as I think of the nearing winter,
And the transient light that gleams like the ghost of May.

The first line of this stanza has the speaker observing 'the umber clouds that drive for the sun', then, in the very next line, he says 'And a sorrow no argument ever can take away / Goes through my heart.'

The speaker is not explicitly saying that the presence of these 'umber clouds' causes the sorrow, but the way one thought follows directly on the heels on the other suggests this might be the case. We notice that option (a) argues that the cause of the speaker's sorrow is 'the umber and so option (a) becomes tempting.

However, as we read on, we are pointed in another direction: 'a sorrow no argument ever can take away / Goes through my heart as I think of the nearing winter'. The word 'as' suggests a causal link between the speaker's thoughts turning to 'the nearing winter' and the 'sorrow'. Given the explicit language used by the speaker, we are forced to go with option (c) instead, as the speaker is pretty much spelling out that the 'impending arrival of winter' is what has caused his sorrow.

As an aside, the reason that the speaker's sorrow is mentioned immediately after the mention of these clouds is almost certainly because these clouds remind the speaker of the impending winter. So, in a sense, the clouds are linked to his sorrow in a roundabout way; nevertheless, option (c) remains a stronger answer than (a).

8. The last two lines of the poem tell us that:

    a) **the blue-tit is unaware that he will soon face mortal danger**
    b) **the poet has seen a hawk that will hunt the blue-tit in winter.**
    c) **the hawk is unaware that it will soon be winter, and that he will then be doomed.**
    d) **the blue-tit is unaware that there is a prophecy that says he will be doomed.**

                                                                                   Answer: A

The correct answer here is (a), since the final two lines of the poem focus on the fact that the blue-tit is unaware of the mortal dangers he will imminently face on winter's arrival.

Let's look at the final stanza in its entirety:

And the bird, unaware, blessing the summer eternal,
Joyfully labouring, proud of his strength, gay-plumed,
Unaware of the hawk and the snow and the frost-bound nights,
And his death foredoomed.

The blue-tit is 'unaware' of the 'hawk and the snow and the frost-bound nights'. These are all things that will threaten the blue-tit's life during the winter, and which present such a potent threat to the blue-tit that its death is almost certain ('death foredoomed'). This tallies closely with how option (a) describes the gist of the final two lines.

Option (d) is trying to trip us up by suggesting that there is a 'prophecy that says [the blue-tit] will be doomed.' This is not correct. Rather, when the speaker says that the blue-tit's death is 'foredoomed', he is using hyperbolic language to emphasise just how treacherous the winter months will be for the blue-tit, and just how small its chances of survival are. There is not a literal prophecy, and so option (d) can be dismissed.

9. The form of this poem is best described as:

   a) five four-line stanzas with no rhyme scheme
   b) a collection of rhyming limericks
   c) five four-line stanzas written in rhyming couplets
   d) five four-line stanzas with the second and fourth line rhyming.

Answer: D

We have already noted previously in this guide that a stanza refers to a paragraph within a poem. There are five stanzas in this poem, and each one is four lines long.

There is also an *abcb* rhyme scheme in each stanza, meaning that the last word of the second and fourth lines rhyme.

Taking all of this together, it is clear that option (d) is correct: there are 'five four-line stanzas with the second and fourth line rhyming.

As an aside, a limerick is a type of comical poem made up of five lines, with an *aabba* rhyme scheme. This poem is clearly not a limerick, however, so we safely dismiss option (b). Nevertheless, I have included a limerick by the poet Edward Lear below, just so you can see what one looks like!

There was an Old Man with a beard,
Who said, "It is just as I feared!—
Two Owls and a Hen,
Four Larks and a Wren,
Have all built their nests in my beard!"

10. Overall the feeling of the poem is best described as:

a) a happy memory from childhood
b) a reflection on the bitter-sweet final moments of autumn
c) a comical reflection on the ignorance of a blue-tit who thinks that he is invincible.
d) a strong argument in favour of daylight saving time.

Answer: B

The feelings a reader derives from a poem is deeply subjective, and the very idea of having to pick an option from a choice of four is (in my opinion!) slightly absurd. That said, this sort of question has appeared many times in 10+ papers – and, as mentioned before, we are not here to debate the examiner on whether their choice of question is valid.

Rather, we want to find the most appropriate answer of the four and score the mark!

Option (a) describes the poem as 'a happy memory from childhood'. We cannot know for sure whether or not this poem is drawn from a memory from the speaker's childhood; however, there is no mention of this being a childhood memory anywhere in the poem, which makes this conclusion deeply speculative, and thus encourages us to approach option (a) with scepticism.

Option (b) describes the poem as 'a reflection on the bitter-sweet final moments of autumn'. There is little doubt that the poem is a reflection on the final moments of autumn. There is also plenty to suggest that the speaker finds these moments bitter-sweet. This period is sweet insofar as nature seems to be rejoicing and the speaker is taking in the beauty of the scene. Equally, it is bitter insofar as the speaker is deeply cognisant of the temporality of this joyous scene.

Option (b), then, is a very fair assessment of the 'overall feeling' of the poem.

Option (c) describes the poem as 'a comical reflection on the ignorance of a blue-tit who thinks that he is invincible.' There is no doubt that the poem does explore the ignorance of a blue-tit, though the blue-tit's ignorance seems more to do with its conviction that summer is eternal as opposed to its conviction that he is invincible.

Moreover, the idea that the poem is a 'comical' reflection also makes option (c) less appealing. Comedy is deeply subjective, and thus it is impossible to categorically say that nobody will find this poem humorous in some way. However, the overall tone of this poem seems to be deeply serious as opposed to humorous.

With all this in mind, option (c) does not seem like an especially convincing assessment of the poem.

Option (d) is the easiest of the four to dismiss. The poem in no way seems to be an 'argument in favour of daylight saving time' – indeed, daylight saving time is never mentioned explicitly or implicitly. Option (d), then, is very plainly incorrect.

Having worked through all four options, (b) stands out as the most credible assessment of the poem – and is, sure enough, the answer the examiner is looking for!

www.ingramcontent.com/pod-product-compliance
Lightning Source LLC
Chambersburg PA
CBHW081619100526
44590CB00021B/3505